To Debbie

Enjoy the Caves

[signature] Sherman

andace 2021

The Crystal Caves

An adventure by
Candace L. Sherman

The Crystal Caves
2018©Copyright Candace L. Sherman

Publisher: Crystal Books

Contact the author at: cls@clsherman.com
Or visit: www.clsherman.com
Book Design: theartoftheword.com

Maybe one day, after centuries,
we can become brilliant gems in crystal caves
and we will be immortal after all."
— *Keelie Breanna*

Amethyst. Purple.
Connects the energy center
found at the top of the head
with intuitive protective
forces. It protects you
against over indulgences
showing you *how* to be
insightful.

Aventurine. Light green
with a sparkly sheen.
Stop your mind from going in
two or more directions at
once to create calm.

Clear Quartz.
Shows you clarity and
beyond. Knowledge from
present and past life can be
stored within. Take a chance—
use it to see where you might
have been and where you
might go now.

Grey Moonstone.
Brings a beacon of light
into dark corners of the
mind and dreams.
It's as if the moon swings
the mind open to shine a
light inside.

Rose Quartz. This light pink stone is for
self-love. Connects the self with your own
heart to know how to care for yourself
first. Come from a place of inner strength
and then assist others. Do not confuse this
with being selfish. There is a huge
difference between being selfish and being
able to take care of yourself.

Pearls. Clockwise: white,
blue, black, and pink.
Please see *Chapter Six* for
details on the amazing
properties of these wonderful
creations of nature.

Bone and Ivory. Off-white.
Absorbs shock to the system both
physically and emotionally. When you
feel bombarded by life and its struggles,
Bone or Ivory is especially useful.

Turquoise. Blue to
green. After shock,
choose the direction
you take with
renewed energy.
The Universe
wants you to move
ahead.

Aquamarine. Blue to bluish green.
Discover what partnership means to you. Inner
partnership comes first, and then sharing your
thoughts becomes important for inner growth.

*You'll find a guide to clearing stone energy as part of
our story on Page 75. There's more information at:
clsherman.com*

How the Adventure Develops

Cast of Characters
In order of appearance

Peter...is an adventuresome lad who feels deeply about almost everything. He is five years old, has lived in one place his whole life, and feels he's the leader of this traveling group of four. Peter has worn hearing aids since he was six months old. Without them, he does not hear the lowest sounds and tones. Maybe because of his hearing difficulties, Peter sees things differently. He has a strong sense of vision both literally and figuratively. He gets frustrated when his travelling companions cannot keep up with his vivid imagination and sense of adventure. On the other hand, he never sees his younger sister as a burden, rather as a companion. When he's nervous, his straight brown hair often stands on end.

Kathy...is Peter's two-and-a-half-year-old sister. She was adopted when she was just ten days old and knows only the family she is now part of. Everyone loves Kathy. She has ash-blonde hair that is usually adorned in mismatched pig-tails. When she smiles, a dimple on one cheek almost glows. It makes everyone else smile and want to share in whatever delight made the dimple stand out.

Gwen…is fourteen years old. She wears leg braces to walk. Sometimes, she sees and feels only her handicap and not her inner radiance—she is truly lovely, inside and out. She isn't sure why she has to spend time with these three children other than their parents are all friends—when the adults gather, so do their kids. Being the eldest of the group, and with natural caretaker instincts, she feels she must act as a babysitter for the group making decisions for them when their parents are not around.

Justine…at only twelve months old is the youngest of the foursome. She is already walking on her own, although she sometimes reverts to crawling for speed! She has not begun to speak yet, and communicates via gurgling and cooing noises. Nonetheless, she observes things the others do not. She has sparkling dark eyes and matching dark hair that is naturally spikey and looks like a punk-rocker cut. Her pointed ears and innocent, adorable face make her appear fairy-like at times.

Each child was given a golden fabric pouch with a simple drawstring closure. Feeling the weight of the pouch, they immediately opened them to find an amethyst crystal inside.

Chapter One:
THE ADVENTURE BEGINS

Peter moved slowly, but with purpose.

The purpose was to provide his three companions with proof that when autumn leaves fell from the trees, they turned into snakes before they hit the ground.

It was a quest that might take some patience on his part. Even though patience was not his strong suit, he remained alert in case his purpose suddenly revealed itself in the form of a venomous legless reptile.

Peter was five. It irritated him that everyone immediately associated his impatience with his age. Was there some unwritten rule that all five year olds were impatient? Here he was, walking the backyard at a pace that everyone could keep up with. Surely that was a sign of patience and camaraderie?

Yes, he was out in front of the lineup, but why shouldn't he be? It was his yard after all!

He turned back to reassure himself that his three companions were keeping up. Peter's two-and-a-half-year-old adopted sister, Kathy, was maintaining the pace surprisingly well.

Close behind her, fourteen-year-old Gwen was carrying one-year-old Justine on her hip.

Peter took a moment to survey his companions.

Would this group all be friends if their three sets of parents weren't?

Having different interests, and being different ages usually had the group at odds with one another. They each had short fuses. Why Peter was singled out as being quick-tempered didn't seem fair to him.

Fifteen minutes earlier, they had all been inside the house.

Given that it was Peter and Kathy's home, and Peter being older, he had been handed the task of entertaining not only his little sister, but their two guests as well.

He had stood in front of the living room window wondering what they could do while their parents sat around the kitchen table drinking coffee and eating zucchini bread.

Previous group adventures included making indoor forts from dining room chairs with household blankets and sheets draped over the backs or chasing around the barn, supposedly feeding the chickens.

It was fall and the leaves were changing color.

Mesmerized by what he saw, it was then that Peter told his friends the falling leaves turned color first, and then became slippery, slimy snakes before they touched ground.

Hearing this struck a note of fear in his three companions. They really did want to play outside. But news of snakes among the leaves made them quickly reconsider that.

But here was their dilemma: Let fear take over and remain safely inside? Or take their chances and go out and play among the brightly colored falling leaves?

A decision was made, and they all headed for the back door.

If they came across snakes, so be it.

With his mighty sword (made of cardboard covered in aluminum foil) tucked inside his belt, Peter felt ready for anything.

Certain they would keep an eye on each other and young Justine especially, their parents relaxed and enjoyed each other's company while the children traipsed outside.

Justine was walking well on her own these days, but still required supervision. She had not begun to talk beyond baby babble, but she seemed to understand what everyone said.

She wanted to be anywhere the other three children were. If they tried to escape her presence, she crawled and walked until she found them.

It was easier to include her, rather than be yelled at by their parents who wanted to be certain she was with them at all times.

Peter felt he had enough on his plate watching his sister, he didn't need another small human to keep watch over. Which meant the task of watching Justine fell mainly to Gwen. And even though Gwen was the eldest, she was, in

Peter's mind, an equal because she, too, was handicapped.

He needed hearing aids. She needed leg braces.

Born with a hole in her heart, Gwen worked so hard at breathing, that her other body muscles never developed as they should. Though the hole was repaired when she was two, her leg muscles still wanted to cave inward when she walked. Wearing braces slowed her down, but she always managed to get where she wanted to be.

Like Peter, she came under the heading of being the same as other children, but different.

Unable to hear the lowest sounds and tones, Peter had worn hearing aids since he was a toddler. Bright 'Kermit the Frog' green in color, the aids covered the whole outside of each ear. Or they were supposed to.

In the excitement of heading out to sneak up on snakes, Peter forgot to put them on—or maybe it was accidently on purpose. Everyone knows a five-year-old boy feels he doesn't have to listen to *girls*.

Peter kept his slow, deliberate pace and they all scanned the ground carefully as they walked. Though finding snakes would be an adventure, they still wanted to make sure they didn't step on any.

The trees that lined the perimeter of the property were brilliant with orange, yellow, green, and red leaves.

Peter liked the idea of gathering them into a big pile and jumping into them.

That would be difficult for Gwen with her leg braces, but she would find a way to join in the fun.

With their eyes on the ground and kicking at the leaves as they went, the cave was suddenly upon them and they almost walked straight into it. Peter and Kathy had lived here all their lives but they had certainly never seen it before.

The entrance was like an enormous open mouth about to swallow them up. Massive purple crystals pointed up and down around the cave opening looking like the teeth of a huge smiling, grape juice-soaked mouth.

Brilliant purple rainbows seem to glisten and reflect off the crystals in the sunlight in marked contrast to the splendor of the autumn foliage.

A sound came from inside the cave. A soft melodic noise that seemed to be calling them, encouraging them to enter.

"Oh, my goodness!" said Gwen with alarm in her voice.

They had prepared themselves for coming across snakes. Being presented with a crystal clustered cave opening... well, they hadn't been expecting that.

Peter was still out in front and was much more excited than the girls.

He'd read every action-packed Spiderman book and comic in existence, and combed through even more exploits about pillaging pirates.

But a cave? A crystal cave! In his own backyard? Now this really *was* an adventure!

Turning to his friends he said very loudly, "Wow! This is exciting. I've never seen this before. And I've been here woads of times!" (Without his hearing aids, Peter didn't realize he was shouting. His speech pattern went off a bit too.)

Gwen put Justine down for a moment and stepped forward to take charge since she was the eldest of the four. Facing Peter, she planted herself firmly in front of him, stood up straight, and put her hand up to stop him.

"Oh, no we don't, Peter. We're not going in there without our parents. Or at least telling them first."

Defiantly, Peter pushed away her hand and walked straight towards the cave. He didn't want any *girl* giving him orders. Kathy followed her brother. Gwen, feeling frustrated that her first serious attempt to rule the others fell short, turned to take Justine's hand. But Justine's enlarged eyes were fixated on the light reflecting off the purple crystals.

And then Gwen saw it.

In this light, Justine looked just like a fairy. Her ears were almost pointy. Her pudgy cheeks were now pink and glowing. Her dark hair set off eyes that sparkled like stars in the sky. She was a shoo-in for the fairies depicted in Gwen's books at home.

Justine's look of excitement as she reached for the crystals almost brought tears to Gwen's eyes.

Feeling stuck between what she thought was her duty to keep the others safe, wanting to please Justine, and have an adventure herself, Gwen wasn't sure what to do. She turned around to see that Peter and Kathy had already entered the cave. She lifted Justine back up onto her hip and followed them in.

Suddenly there was a rush and whoosh of air. And without warning, the mouth of the cave closed firmly behind them.

Turning quickly, they tried to push the cave wall where the opening had been. Try as they might, no exit could be found. No matter how hard they pushed, nothing moved. The doorway was now non-existent.

Nevertheless, it was light in here.

The crystals glowed like brightly burning lamps illuminating several tunnels that led in different directions off the main cave.

Turning around and around, they tried to decide which way to go to get back to the relative safety of the backyard, snakes among the leaves notwithstanding.

Suddenly a man appeared out of nowhere. He was dressed like someone from ancient times. He was wearing a white toga and carried a rolled-up scroll in his right hand. A gold leaf crown sat upon his head. He had a kindly face. Smiling, he looked at each of the four children and asked, "Are you lost?"

Even though they had never seen a man in a dress, much less one that had only one shoulder strap, they all somehow felt he was here to help.

In stories they'd read, the good guys were always dressed in white, so they assumed toga-man must be a good guy too!

They immediately surrounded him, all speaking at once. It sounded like the babble of monkeys at the zoo, getting louder and louder. No one child could be understood above the other.

Holding up his left hand as if to say stop, the man smiled patiently. The children got the hint and quickly became quiet, allowing Peter alone to speak.

"There was an opening into the cave. That's how we got here. Now it's gone and we don't know how to get out. Can you show us?"

"Didn't you all want an adventure today?" asked the man. They looked sheepishly at one another and began to shrug their shoulders. "You chose to enter the cave," he continued. "Now an adventure is exactly what the cave has in store for you. On this journey, you will learn and discover things you didn't know before."

He suddenly spoke more firmly.

"Please pay attention as I say this. In order to leave the cave, you must work with one another as friends who *all* have an equal say." Looking directly at the youngest of the group, he smiled. "Even Justine has an equal say in here.

I know she has not been walking long, nor has she really begun to speak, but she is to be included as an *equal*."

The four of them nodded that they understood what the man had said and would do as he suggested.

After a moment of silence, Peter spoke again. "But why did the door kwose?"

"The doorway you came through is gone for now, Peter, because *now* is the time to examine the strengths and weaknesses you each have. Inside the caves, you must learn how to use your strengths and cope with the weaknesses within yourselves, as well as one another. You'll learn how your strengths can help you carefully choose which tunnels to take, and eventually you will find your way out."

Before the children had a chance to fully digest what he was suggesting, he went on.

"Your first lesson is one of how to leave the weakness of *overindulgence* behind. Overindulgences occur when you have too much of something. Like when you eat too much cake, and end up with a tummy ache. Too much of anything, food, drink, talking too much, are all forms of overindulgences. Even an overload of emotions can be a form of indulgence. If you're feeling sorry for yourself for entering the cave with no way out as yet, that is a form of overindulgence too."

Obviously confused, the four exchanged glances. Peter asked the question they were all thinking. "How do we know you really *are* trying to help us?"

"Guess you don't know that, Peter. I can tell you that I am here to help, but only you as individuals can decide if I am, in fact, here for that or not."

Peter turned to his friends and began to ask them what they thought, whether they should trust this strange toga-clad man when Gwen spoke out. It had dawned on her that she heard something a few times now, and needed an answer. "How do you know his name is Peter, or her name is Justine?"

"Good question, Gwen. I have all your names here on my scroll."

He unrolled the scroll and showed them their names displayed in bold, gold letters.

They were all astounded and even more confused by this. Moving closer together, they felt a bit more secure. Though their minds were jumbled and they were scared, they knew on some inner level they must continue to ask questions.

Whispering together, the four children encouraged Peter to continue being the spokesperson for them all.

"Do you mean in order to move ahead, it's wike a game? That each time we wearn something, it brings us kwoser to the doorway to home?"

"Actually, Peter, that's not a bad way to look at your adventure. You could say that this journey is like a board game. You will learn different things, and as you do, you will choose a tunnel. That tunnel will be like a roll of the dice, and then you move ahead. However, I will not tell you which tunnel is the one that leads home. Your adventure begins here in the purple amethyst cavern where you will learn about the overindulgences I was just talking about."

"What's amethyst?" asked Peter.

"Amethyst is the stone that's all around you right now."

Almost on cue, the walls began to sparkle with purple light. It was as though the cave walls had turned into millions of cones of purple cotton candy, and the spun sugar was glistening in sunlight. But there wasn't any sunlight in this cave. Instead, the light came from deep inside the crystals.

"Amethyst is a form of quartz crystal, a rock source formed from volcanic actions that happened thousands of years ago. Back in dinosaur times. Although amethyst is a purple colored quartz, you'll notice some crystals also have clear and white tones in them. Shades of purple vary in amethyst depending upon what other elements were present when the volcanic action took place. There are many stones that are part of the quartz group, such as opal, jasper, and agates, to name a few.

"Here's the important part. All stones have healing properties. What that means is that stones can assist you in some way if you tune into their energy. The minerals found in stones can cause a reaction to your emotions, and sometimes to your physical bodies as well. Just as food can cause a reaction in your body."

The children were spellbound.

"Let me explain a bit more how amethyst works. As I mentioned, amethyst is part of the quartz family. Quartz helps provide clarity. In ancient Greek and Roman times, when people dressed like me and drank wine daily, amethyst was used the night before soldiers went to battle. They drank from special goblets that had amethyst mounted in them. Because the amethyst provided clarity, and importantly, protected from overindulgence, they would have clear heads to do their best in battle the next day.

"Amethyst was also viewed in ancient times to be a sign of power and many religious men wore rings made with it. More than that though, amethyst helps connect your crown chakra—the energy center found at the top of your head— with intuitive protective forces, which show you how to be insightful. This will be helpful if you are to find your way through the cave. Does this make sense to you all?"

The four looked at one another, confused. Noses crinkled up. At this moment, they weren't even sure how to ask questions. The non-response was an answer for this Greek/Roman scholar—or whatever he was! He smiled broadly, making them feel more relaxed. He was enjoying their company. He pressed on.

"Understand this...when you connect with amethyst properly, you can figure out what direction you might take in the cave...and in life. You will also be protected from overindulgent emotions like panic—something that can happen easily inside the cave, especially when you think there's no way out."

Nods of heads told him each child seemed to have a grasp of the concept of the stone energy.

And then a strange thing happened.

Each child felt physically warm with this new knowledge and they experienced a gradual calming. The tension that had been gripping their shoulders was now letting go.

It was then that their new friend unexpectedly and magically bestowed a golden fabric pouch with a simple drawstring closure upon each child.

Feeling the weight of the pouch, they opened the closure to find an amethyst crystal inside. The coolness of the crystal in their hands held them momentarily speechless. As they slowly placed the crystal back in their pouch, they looked up to discover toga-man had disappeared.

The children spun around on themselves. Had he simply moved to another place in the cavern? Looks of panic came over their faces.

He was not there.

Calling out for him was useless. How could they when

they didn't know his name?

Peter's shoulders went up towards his ears, and like the others, he felt scared. "Guess we are awone again. Let's think about which way to go."

There was no discussion.

The four friends looked at once towards the opening farthest away. They didn't stop to question why they had all chosen the same tunnel opening.

Maybe they all felt comfortable continuing on in the purple glow this tunnel provided.

Even though this might lead them further into the cave, they headed into that tunnel without hesitation.

The ground underfoot was smooth. Perfect for each child's walking ability.

Gwen's handicap and Justine's limited endurance meant walking would be slow if they were to remain together as a group.

Their desire for safety in numbers kept them together. Being closer in age and height, Kathy took Justine's hand this time, their heads were close together. They all fell silent, each to their own thoughts.

What would be next on this adventure?

Where would this tunnel lead? Would it take them home to their parents?

Would they ever see their parents again?

None of the children knew the answers. They just knew

they had to press on.

And so they moved further into the purple glow of the tunnel. Not knowing what might await them.

*Turning around slowly, they were stunned
to be facing a nine-foot tall giraffe.*

Chapter Two:
DON'T GO CRAZY

The now comforting purple glow that accompanied them through the tunnel started to become tinged with green.

They had not altered their path, so why had the color changed?

Their already slow pace slowed even more.

Nervously, they craned their necks and saw there was another cave coming up.

Stopping just short of entering this new cave, they looked inside to make sure it was safe.

There was nothing in the open space, nothing at all, so they walked forward. They gazed in wonder at the gentle green light that flooded the cavern.

Once again, leading off the main cave were tunnel openings. Hoping one would lead home, they spread out to the edge of the cave to investigate, each peering towards the tunnel they had chosen without going any further.

Their backs were turned towards the center when they suddenly felt hot breath on each of their necks.

Turning around slowly, they were stunned to be facing a nine-foot tall giraffe.

All necks went into awkward positions trying to see all the way up to its head. Their already stressed shoulders tightened even further. Gwen struggled to keep her balance.

The giraffe blinked her long-lashed eyes and spoke in a low, almost undetectable lady-like voice. "Welcome to my cave. I see you have arrived unscathed by your adventure so far."

Without his hearing aids, Peter couldn't hear a thing the giraffe was saying. Becoming flustered, he began to yell for everyone to tell him what he was missing! His hair seemed to stand on end with annoyance.

Gwen took over.

Stepping in front of the giraffe, she motioned with her right hand in a backward wave to indicate that Peter should step to the rear. She put her finger to her lips and told him firmly to "Shhh."

Gwen had this one covered.

And though he was clearly upset, Peter decided to let Gwen take over. He huddled with Kathy and Justine and got out of the way of this newly found giant.

A talking giraffe!

The youngsters' eyes were as big as saucers, not knowing what to expect next.

How did a giraffe get in here without any one of them noticing it entering? For that matter, how did a giraffe get inside the cave? Yes, this cavern was high enough for it to stand upright. But the tunnels were not so high. Even on its knees, the giraffe couldn't have crawled through!

Fearlessly, Gwen stood in front of the giraffe. Seemingly

capable of anything, nothing was holding her back from confronting this creature.

You would never know she was handicapped with leg braces. Never able to run and play as normal children with strong legs, Gwen missed out on a physically demanding childhood. Perhaps that's why in situations such as these, she had more of an adult-like quality.

Her fair brown hair almost glistened as she stood in front of this animal. It was as though the green radiance of the cave bounced light off her head to create a halo effect.

Her friends noticed it, but they kept quiet. This was an important moment. They didn't want to disturb her. Gwen was about to speak to a talking giraffe.

Gwen's olive skin tone almost matched the spots on the giraffe. It was as if of all the group, she was the one that had something in common with the giraffe, that she was definitely the one to lead this conversation.

Gwen waved her left hand at the giraffe as if to say, "Hi."

They seemed to smile at one another.

This spotted giant lowered and raised her head between a bent position as if studying this young woman standing bravely in front of her, and standing erect like the proud creature she was.

Gwen opted to stand still until the giraffe spoke again.

"You have come into my cave on a quest for knowledge."

"Honestly, we came here trying to find our way out of the cave, to get home. Can you help us figure which way we ought to go?"

The giraffe continued in a whisper. "You came here, and are asking to leave right away? Don't be rude. You have come into my home. At least let us talk a bit before you move on. Why are you in such a hurry, anyway? We have not yet begun what we must learn together."

Feeling suddenly betrayed by who knows what, Gwen responded a bit indignantly.

"Learn? All we want to learn is how to get back home."

Choosing to ignore the attitude from Gwen, the giraffe simply blinked her long lashes again and continued.

"First, let me share that in the giraffe kingdom, we do not have leaders in our groups, or herds if you will."

She motioned with her giant head towards Peter (who now had Kathy holding tightly onto the back of his belt, who in turn had Justine in a sitting position gripping her ankles.)

Fear had such a hold on these three, that with each breath the giraffe took, they no longer saw spots, but rather one big brown blur.

"I know Peter cannot hear the low tone I chose to speak to you with. For now, he needs to let you be up front. It's important for you all to learn from the lifestyle of a giraffe while here in my cavern."

Not budging from her spot in front of the giraffe, no one knew if Gwen was afraid and not showing it, or the bravest person they ever met.

Shifting her attitude, Gwen spoke with a new sense of calm. "What is it about your lifestyle that we are supposed to learn? And why is it more important than us getting out of here?"

It never occurred to Gwen, or her companions, to ask how it was that the giraffe spoke perfect English.

"We never leave our young behind. We take turns watching out for the youngest members of our herd. We do not fight over territory when provoked. Instead, we opt to move on to a new place. If we are seriously attacked, we will kick our attackers, but normally we choose to live in a quiet way, working together with our herd-mates. When we walk, we move the two legs on the same side of our bodies, and then switch. It confuses would-be assailants as to whose legs belong to whom. When we run, we shift, and use our two front legs together, and swing our rear legs outside the front legs to remain in balance. We use our height, and great eyesight, to keep an eye on our neighbors, observe what they are doing, and determine who might be heading our way. That way we know if danger is approaching. It gives us enough time to decide what to do. Mainly, we are a breed of animal that work together to get where we need to feed and find water. Emotionally, we try to not lose patience with one another. Instead, we connect the dots in our minds to create an emotional balance. We also have huge hearts that assist us in staying in tune with one another. You four need to learn all this in order to go forward in my cave. Please share this information with Peter now. The others have heard what I said, though fear has momentarily prevented them from fully understanding it. It will be good for them to hear this again as you repeat it for Peter."

Turning back to the others, Gwen shared the giraffe's story.

Peter became impatient.

He had very clear thoughts each and every day of what he wanted to do, and where he wanted to go. Having someone tell him he ought to work together with the other three members of the herd might be a good thought, but not one he wanted to hear.

After all, didn't they come on this adventure because he suggested it?

Didn't they enter the cave because he wanted to?

Didn't they come into the cave without adults?

Doesn't this sound like something an adult might say?

With a shake of his shoulders, he shrugged off the two girls who were still holding onto him and kicked at the dirt floor. The sudden action made Kathy fall on her bottom while Justine rolled on the floor of the cave.

Kathy looked up at her older brother and spoke with

caring in her voice.

"Peter, why are you upset? Don't you want to stay with us girls?"

Gwen pleaded with him. "Peter, we came into the cave at your request for an adventure. We are all here together. Now it feels like you don't want to be with us. The giraffe is saying we all need to work together. Doesn't that mean you have to give us your input on where we ought to go?"

With Gwen's plea, it seemed the real meaning of the giraffe's story had suddenly dawned on him.

Now he understood.

Peter looked at his sister and Gwen, and became brighter in spirit almost instantly. He could see that Kathy was actually shaking with fear making her blonde, mismatched pigtails bob around in time to her shaking shoulders.

Peter reached out to steady her and smiled.

"I was just upset because I felt weft out. That giraffe spoke too soft for me to hear. That's all. We can work together to move on. That's a good thing." Then in a whisper, he asked Gwen, "How is it you aren't afwaid? That giraffe is so big!"

"Peter, I have grown up around horses. They're pretty big animals too. My grandmother loves giraffes, so I have always seen pictures of them around her house. She even watches programs on TV about giraffes. Guess I don't think they are any different than horses with longer legs and necks. Either that, or it's an age thing. I am older, so I have seen more than you."

That last comment felt like a dig to Peter. He was on the verge of snapping again when Kathy pulled on his belt. He decided not to give into his emotions and stood still.

Justine came out from behind Kathy so she could get a good look at this giant giraffe. She smiled up at it, and the giraffe bent over to get a closer look at Justine. The giraffe's warm breath seemed to radiate heat all over her.

Justine's tiny right hand went out in front of her, and the giraffe stuck its nose in it.

Justine giggled.

Gwen didn't.

She leapt forward to grab Justine out of possible harm's way. In turn, Peter grabbed Gwen by the waist. Peter whispered a warning: "Don't move too qwickly, or she could be in twouble."

A look of panic came over Gwen but she heeded Peter's warning. She stood perfectly still, but made sure she was still within arm's reach of Justine.

Justine and the giraffe exchanged glances—they had a moment and understood one another. The giraffe lifted its massive head. Gwen slid her hands slowly around the little girl's shoulders, and Justine backed away to her friends, fully intact.

Gwen breathed a sigh of relief.

The group turned to the giraffe again, this time, united. Now they were working together. The giraffe smiled. Lesson learned.

The children felt their golden pouches get heavier.

They reached into their pouches to find a new stone inside. A green one. Looking at one another for a second and then back up at the giraffe, they ask in unison, "What's this?"

"It's called aventurine, it's also part of the quartz family."

Gwen spoke up. "This stone is not anything like the amethyst we got earlier. We were told *that* was part of the quartz family."

The giraffe lowered her head and was still speaking softly, but she was close enough to Peter that he could hear and understand this time.

"Quartz is one of the largest groupings of stones known on this planet. You will hear of many stones that are part of the quartz family over time, so don't be surprised. What is different with this green stone is not only the color and opaqueness, which means it has a lack of see-through quality, but also the energy unique to it. Aventurine helps balance your emotions, so you don't go crazy. As an example, with so many choices to make on this journey of yours, you could break down and cry with the fear of never finding your way out of the cave. There are also times in life when you feel two different ways at the same time, like when you want to go in two directions at once.

"While you are in this cave, part of you knows you chose to have an adventure, and you need to take action in order to find your way home. There can also be a part of you that feels you want to remain where you are right now, and make the universe magically take you home. At times like that, you may feel there's a battle going on inside your head. Hold on to the aventurine. Calm your emotions. As long as you work together and respect each other's abilities, you will make good choices, and achieve your goal...without battle."

The giraffe now focused on Peter specifically. He squirmed a bit, afraid of what might come next.

"I see you wore your sword into the cave today, Peter. Let's hope you do not have need of it. Remember: you are all equal. You alone don't have to do battle for everyone."

The giraffe had studied the faces of these four children as she spoke. She was ready to dismiss them.

"I think you understand what I have shared with you about this stone's energy, as well as how giraffes live. I have enjoyed our time together. Now tell me, which way are you going to leave my cavern?"

They looked at the tunnel options. Only one seemed to be the same green color as the stone they had in their hands. Just as they had chosen the purple opening to lead them from the amethyst cave, instinctively, they began to move towards the green opening.

They stopped to see if the giraffe agreed with them, only to realize she was no longer in the cave.

She had disappeared just as suddenly as toga-man in the first cavern.

They all laughed.

They were beginning to feel like it was normal for these caves to have beings appear and then disappear.

Chuckling, they headed into the tunnel bathed in green light.

A dazzling, clear quartz crystal appeared.
Long and pointed at one end, it bound
itself to the dream catcher's willow circle.

Chapter Three:
CLARITY

The green tunnel seemed to go on forever.

The group stuck together and supported each other just as the giraffe had instructed. Still, the tunnel dragged on.

Right when they were about to give up hope, the children noticed a bright white light up ahead. Optimistic that what they were seeing was daylight, they moved quickly and excitedly towards it.

"Look. There must be an opening ahead," said Kathy. "I can see sunbeams."

"That's what they mean by the light at the end of the tunnel," said Peter positively.

But then…

No one had noticed the misty cloud move in and surround them until it was too late.

Everyone came to a full stop.

Visibility was down to an arm's length in any direction.

"Where has the sunshine gone?" exclaimed Kathy. "Why is this cloud here?"

Gwen said, "This can't be a cloud. Clouds are in the sky. We're in a cave, remember?"

"Then what is it?" Peter asked.

Gwen answered, "Fog. I think it could be fog. When cold moist air hits the warm ground, fog is made. We just had a lesson in school on it. But if it is fog, where is the cool air coming from? Maybe there *is* an opening close by. Should we keep walking?"

"I don't want to walk any further into the fog," said Kathy and crossed her arms to make her point.

Justine sat down on the ground while everyone was trying to figure out what their next move would be.

Aware that they were not alone, they watched wide-eyed as a familiar-looking figure emerged out of the mist.

He had baggy pants, a blousy shirt, scruffy face hair, and an odd black hat. But it was his wooden leg that gave him away.

"You're a pirate!" Peter exclaimed. Peter stepped towards him, sword drawn at the ready.

"Hey, hey, there yungins," said the pirate in that piratey, singsong way of greeting.

Kathy and Gwen stepped back. Pirates were *not* to be trusted!

Peter waved his sword towards the pirate. His boldness caught the pirate off-guard and the crooked smile momentarily disappeared from his face. In the hazy light of the fog the aluminum foil sword looked more like a real sword with weird markings.

But you can't fool a pirate and he played along.

"Arrgghh, mateys, there's no need to attack me! I'm here ta give yaw a gifft."

Lowering his tinfoil sword, Peter seemed interested in what the pirate might have to offer. They had already received two gifts. An amethyst and an aventurine. Maybe this pirate had something good as well.

"I gots me here a treasure map."

The pirate pulled a scrap of paper from deep in a pocket. The paper was soft and dirty from being folded and refolded so often. Watching the four children through thick, bushy eyebrows, he spoke in a low whisper as if not to be heard by other people secretly listening in.

"Dis map leads right to da treasure. Yous just have ta folla me."

"What is the treasure?" Peter wanted to know.

"Well, matey, there's a good question. What would yer like fer a treasure?"

Boldly now, Peter stood with his chest high and exclaimed, "Gold, of course!"

Holding the map in his right hand, the pirate stuck out his left towards Peter and displayed a shiny gold coin.

"Like dis ya mean?"

Peter leaned forward to get a closer look. "I've never seen a coin like *that* before."

"Dis here's a doubloon, yungster. I stole it yars ago. Gots it from a ship I did, that were sailing to da Americas from Spain. We attacked, and won. This were just one of da spoils we gots. And this here map will lead ya right ta the cave where I gots the rest. Ya want da map? Y is jes gots ta folla me down this tunnel and I'll give it ta ya. This tunnel...rights here."

Through the fog they could barely see the opening he was pointing to.

Peter started to follow the pirate but was stopped by Gwen's frantic yell of, "NO!"

Turning quickly, Peter's eyes met Gwen's gaze.

Gwen stepped forward and spoke firmly. "Remember, Peter, our goal is to go home. We are supposed to work together. I for one, do not want to go with this...this *pirate* for any reason. And since I do not agree, we are *not* going to follow him. No matter how much gold he says he has."

This was the second time Gwen had stopped Peter from doing what he wanted. Unhappily, Peter replaced his sword into his belt. Though he didn't want to admit it, Gwen was right. Again.

Looking at the pirate he said, "Listen mister, we have to agree on which tunnels to take while we're in this cave. That's what we were told to do. Guess your treasure will have to wait for someone else. Sorry."

Peter stepped back to his companions.

With that, the fog around them evaporated. The cool air left the tunnel. And like the fog, the pirate had evaporated as well. He simply was no longer there!

Shrugging of shoulders and raised eyebrows among the

friends let each other know they had no idea what just happened.

In all the excitement, and with the fog lifted, they realized they had lost their bearings. Now they had to decide which was the proper way forward.

Low gurgling sounds made everyone look down at Justine. She hadn't moved since the fog rolled in.

What was she trying to communicate?

They then realized she had sat down facing the direction they were traveling before the pirate showed up. She stretched out a little hand and pointed forward. Without the use of words, her gurgling had given them the confidence to continue on. They were soon moving in the right direction once more. And soon, they could see the white light in the distance again.

Gwen began to sing.

"A sailor went to sea, sea, sea. To see what he could see, see, see. And all that he could see, see, see…"

They all joined in.

"Was the big, blue, sea, sea, sea."

Even Justine gurgled along in time with the others.

It felt good to sing.

Singing as loud as possible made the children's voices echo in the tunnel. Hearing their voices carry was magical. That encouraged them to keep singing. And keep walking. Peter was almost yelling out the song. It made his chest puff out, and he felt like he was back in control. Between the collective singing and the harmonizing echoes, they were together again as a unit and that was all that mattered.

It was Gwen who had started it. She was good like that. Singing always made her feel better. Unable to swing from trees, play dodge ball, or play hide-and-go-seek, she found solace in music instead. Singing kept her heart happy, and her mind occupied. Today, she felt like she had brought her troubled friends a moment of peace and that made her heart fill with pride.

Traveling on, the group approached the edge of the next opening.

Disappointment took over their happy hearts.

They stopped singing when they realized this was not a doorway with sunlight shining through as they had hoped.

Instead, it was another cavern where a lot of white light seemed trapped.

As with the two previous caves, even more tunnel openings led from this open space.

Nervous thoughts of what could possibly be next replaced their light hearts.

Standing quietly in a circle in the middle of the cave, a bright flash of white light threw them off balance, and there he was.

An American Indian.

Standing tall in the center of the group, he wore a tan

deerskin outfit. His shirt was long and straight. His leggings were made of the same cloth. He wore matching moccasins.

His headband of black-tipped white feathers with the base of the shafts wrapped in red wool cascaded all the way down his back. He was holding more black-tipped feathers in one hand.

Yes. He looked exactly like the Indians in those old Western movies and TV shows. Peter immediately thought that he must be some sort of leader, probably a chief, what with all the white feathers on his headdress. Unlike the pirate, and the fearsome image sometimes painted of Indians in movies, he felt safe.

Kathy even ran up to him as if he was a long-lost friend. He smiled at her.

She had a dimple on one cheek that stood proud whenever she smiled, and it was almost glowing right now.

There was an undeniable connection between the two.

Words were unnecessary. They were lost in one another momentarily.

When he looked up at the rest of the travelers, he greeted them each by name.

Just like in school during roll call, they nodded their heads as their name was spoken aloud. They knew what to do, though they did not know why.

As their name was spoken, they sat cross-legged on the ground in front of the Indian.

Gwen sat down carefully. Once on the ground, her legs with their braces needed to be straight out in front of her. There. Now she was comfortable.

"You have done well my friends," said the Indian. "The pirate was a test. He was not someone you ought to be fooled into going with. His map would have lead you in a false direction. As you now know, the tunnels in these caves are important. Which one you choose is part of your lesson. You did well not to follow him. Now it is my turn to teach you about...dream catchers."

The children looked at one another.

They had no idea what a dream catcher was.

The Indian smiled and began his story.

"Long ago, a great Lakota tribal leader had a vision. He saw a hoop form out of a willow branch. The circle became complete when tied together with horsehair. Inside that willow branch circle was a great teacher spirit appearing in the form of a spider. While the spider spun a web inside this willow hoop, he spoke about good and bad forces that come to you throughout life. These energies try to steer you in certain directions. Good powers will work to guide you in the right direction. Bad forces will try to direct you in the wrong direction."

Motioning with his hands like the conductor of an orchestra, the willow hoop he was describing appeared in mid-air, suspended in front of them. It was semi-transparent, like a hologram.

The children were amazed. The Indian continued.

"The spider told the Lakota leader: 'This willow hoop will be called a dream catcher, and is something to hang over your bed for protection while sleeping. The web helps catch good dream messages in order to give you a possible new path to follow in life. If you notice, there is a hole in the center of the web. This releases the bad, or negative forces out into the universe.' When the spider was finished weaving the web and telling his story, the great Lakota leader saw white feathers magically attach themselves to the outer edge of the willow branch circle. They hung down from the willow and waved slowly in the breeze. The Lakota leader instinctively knew the feathers would brush away the bad forces that linger around us all.

"Next, a dazzling, clear quartz crystal appeared. Long and pointed at one end, it also bound itself to the willow circle. Clear quartz helps you see where you have been, and where you might choose to go. Clarity is then brought to your dream messages."

The Indian paused to let this sink in. Satisfied the children were understanding his message, he went on.

"Clear quartz and the clarity it gives to dream messages can help you see and feel the great spirits that are around us all. Some people call them angels. Some refer to these spirits as relatives, or ancestors who have passed over into the great beyond. There are times when people call that feeling of a presence as being around God. It doesn't matter if you pray to God, to many gods, to angels, or to spirits. What does matter are what choices you make from the information you feel you have been given.

"Ultimately, it is up to you to make decisions each and every day, just as you did when you came into these caves. It's also important that you all understand that each and every one of you matter. Even people you might not care for, or people who are bullies matter as well. They all offer you chances to look at life a bit differently and make choices based on what you learn. All experiences, good and bad, offer opportunities to grow."

The Indian wove his mesmerizing story like the Lakota leader's spider weaving his web.

"Clear quartz can be used in many ways. I have shown you one with a dream catcher in relation to dream messages. Now you will learn what else is possible. Coming through the fog as you just did, you eliminated the fog in your brain to see a clearer path in front of you. That brought you here instead of following the pirate.

"To reward your good choice and further your clarity of thinking, you each now have a dream catcher in your pouch to help you dream well in the future. Hang it over your bed and place your bed so your head is in the north. Dream messages that come through with your head to the north usually contain more truth, and have more clarity."

Perplexed looks came over each child as they wondered what direction was north in their bedrooms!

"Some clear quartz crystals have a shadow inside. If that shadow appears to be a figure of sorts, then you have a crystal that is called a phantom. These are also very special quartz stones as the phantom can move over time. You'll remember the phantom being in one place one time, then when you look again, it has moved. I share this to let you know there is magic in stones…get to know them and you'll relate to stones in a new way.

"Clear quartz is full of possibilities, but please, don't be quick to grab hold of someone else's stone. Respect that the energy from *that* person's stone is connected to *that* person. Keep your own stone for your own personal energy. Give respect to stones, and they will respect you as well."

Reaching for their pouches, the four children found they did indeed each now have their very own dream catcher. As they looked up to thank him, the Indian had disappeared into thin air.

Kathy looked bewildered. Somehow, it was as though she loved that Indian.

Kathy was *all* about love.

Her heart was open to all who come across her path. Her world existed to enjoy people as they are, deep inside, where love lives honestly.

"In my head, he told me he had to go now," she said sadly. "That we alone have to choose which path to follow. He is certain our path will be the *right one* since we chose not to follow the pirate."

Kathy opened her pouch and pulled out the crystals and the dream catcher. She laid them on the ground in the order they had been given.

Amethyst was on the left. Aventurine in the middle. The dream catcher with its clear quartz and clarity of thinking on the right. She pointed her index finger at each stone while counting. "One, two, free."

Closing her eyes, she placed her hand over each stone and felt the power of the gifts again.

"Right is right," she suddenly said without explanation and put the gifts back in her pouch.

There were five possible tunnels to enter.

Standing up, Kathy turned and faced the opening on the far left-hand side. Again, she counted out loud. "One, two, free."

(Though her command of language was far more developed than most two-and-a-half year olds, Kathy still counted differently.)

"Yes. Right is right," she said again, more decisively this time with a serious nod of her head. She began to walk towards that third tunnel.

As she did, the entrance lit up with a gray beam of light.

Without questioning the color of the light coming from the cave, or her choice, the other three travelers proceeded to follow her.

*W*hen their eyes focused on the ceiling of the cave,
they saw a very large gray, moon face talking to them.

Chapter Four:
LUNAR ENERGY

This tunnel was even longer than the green tunnel.

It was damp.

The overall light in the tunnel was muted gray and seeing the ground was a bit tricky.

The four young adventurers found themselves walking through mud. Gray, slippery mud. This really slowed down their progress and they moaned as their feet slipped with each new step. As they got more and more stuck in the mud, their moans got louder.

Justine wasn't walking well enough yet to stay balanced in these conditions and started to crawl to keep moving. Within minutes her clothes were covered in mud. Wet and heavy. She came to a stop and began to cry.

Gwen looked around and threw her arms up in the air. She wailed out loud, "My legs are so coated and heavy with mud, I can hardly lift them to keep walking. Between the mud and my leg braces, I am having serious trouble. I can't carry Justine as well."

Peter let out a loud frustrated, "Geesh!" as if to say, "*Girls!*"

Gwen got his meaning and lost her temper. "And why are we here anyway? Peter, this is all your fault."

Even in the dim gray light of the tunnel, the anguish on

Peter's face was visible. Through clenched teeth he growled back at her, "What are you saying?"

Justine's tears were rolling down her chubby pink cheeks. She was crying uncontrollably. No one knew what to do about that. Or anything for that matter.

Shouting to be heard over Justine, Gwen passed blame. "You heard me. It's your fault we came into this awful place with no way out. You *had* to enter the cave, didn't you? We then felt obligated to come with you. Now we can't get home. Do you think we will ever find our way back out?"

Not waiting for an answer, she continued to rail at him. "I think not. We have no idea how long we've even been inside this place. I think we are going to be in here forever and ever. We'll never see daylight again." She paused. "And we'll never see our parents again!"

Gwen's last statement prompted Kathy to burst into tears as well. She sobbed and sobbed.

Peter grimaced. For a split second he was unsure what to say. He was about to yell back at Gwen when he heard a sound off to the side. It was then he saw an opening appear in the tunnel wall.

Straining to see inside this new opening, he couldn't believe what was there.

Impossibly, he saw a huge green pickle with a mouth and eyes looking back at him.

He really didn't want to look away, but turned to see if

his friends had seen it as well.

They had.

Justine and Kathy stopped crying. They had seen something looming up behind the pickle.

"It's a big triangle!" Kathy exclaimed.

They looked past the pickle.

"Well, yes and no," said Gwen. "It's...a pyramid."

They walked just a few cautious steps to the opening and their eyes went up, and up to the very tip of the stone pyramid.

"Wow" Peter exclaimed. "How did that get in here? I wonder if we could cwimb it."

Not waiting for an answer, he plodded with his mud-laden feet further into open space towards the pyramid.

Sticking her hand in front of him, Gwen screamed, "I've had it with you, Peter. We are hungry. We are tired. We are stuck in this mud, and yet here you go off in yet another direction We know nothing about! How dare you put us all in harm's way yet one more time!"

Her voice had gone up an octave or two.

Stopping in his tracks, Peter was surprised by the force of Gwen's rantings.

Kathy stepped forward and pushed Gwen at the hips as hard as she could. "That's my brother. Stop yelling at him."

Justine began crying again, even louder than before.

Instead of railing back at Gwen, Peter turned to Justine and yelled at her.

"Stop crying!"

All four were ankle deep in mud. Frustrated, each of them felt terribly alone.

This was when the giant pickle began to speak. You could have knocked them all over with one of the Indian's feathers. Yes, they had seen that the pickle had a mouth, but who thinks of a pickle actually speaking?

"You are not having a good go of it, are you?"

Their own mouths had dropped open. Kathy put her hands on her hips as if to say, 'No, we're not!" Her pig tails were bobbing like they were connected to a spring.

Justine, who was now sitting up in the mud, stopped her crying and paid attention.

"To say you have got yourselves into a *giant pickle* is stating the obvious."

Chuckling at his own sense of humor, the pickle waited for everyone else to laugh at the joke.

No one did.

"You four seem to have already forgotten the healing stone lessons you have been learning while in the caves."

Looking at them one by one, the pickle waited for a response that didn't come.

No one spoke.

Then suddenly, confused voices were speaking all at once

with excited energy.

"We're lost."

"We don't have food or water."

"We're never going to see our parents again!"

"There's no doorway out."

"We're tired."

"We're dirty."

Justine's forceful baby babbling made it clear that she too, was quite fired up.

"The feelings of despair you are individually experiencing are having a ripple effect. In other words, your frustration is contagious and you're passing that frustration on to the next person. Anger promotes anger. Fear promotes fear. If you had paid attention to the lessons you were given in each cave so far, there would be *no* ripple effect. You would not be upset with each other right now."

He gave them a moment to digest what he was saying, then went on.

"In the first cave, you learned how to not overindulge. That lesson seems lost right now—you are overindulging in anger towards one another. In the second cave, you learned how to not go crazy with so many choices of which tunnel to take. That lesson is quite lost as well. Third, the American Indian shared with you how to have clarity, to catch the good, and let the bad flow through the hole in the web of life to end up out in space.

"Right here and now you are experiencing your first serious challenge in the mud. Especially little Justine who can no longer walk. Look at her! She is absolutely stuck in the mud. Then, Gwen's leg braces are all glopped up. Instead of helping one another, you have resorted to crying, yelling, blame, frustration, and anger. And now, *none* of you can cope."

Feeling attacked by what the pickle was saying, they wanted to defend their actions. They started yelling in unison. Once again, no one child could be heard over the other.

Not having arms or hands to gesture for the children to just *quiet down*, the pickle had no choice but let them wear themselves out with their verbal onslaught. When they finally did stop, he began again with a smile.

"Guess you didn't like what I said."

Sheepish looks appeared on all faces. Their heads hung down in shame. The silence among them spoke volumes.

"Think back over each cave you entered. Remember what was told to you. Think about what you carry in your pouches because of what was shared with you in those caves. Your pouches have stones that can assist when you feel you have issues. Yet here you are, covered with mud that is weighing you down. Not one of you thought to pull out a stone and work with it to find peace, or an emotional direction.

"The gifts you have gained thus far are for a reason. Each one suits a purpose when you find yourselves in a tough emotional place. If you do not learn your lessons, and use these gifts from Mother Earth, then you may never find your way in the tunnels...or in life. There are gifts for each of you in life, well beyond the stones contained within your new pouches. Make use of any and all tools the universe has to offer. You will then find your way."

This last declaration finally had the children paying attention.

The pickle continued. "Mark my words, I am appearing to you for a specific reason. Think about it. I am a very large pickle. You didn't laugh at my little joke. I understand you don't feel like laughing right now, but as I said, you have gotten yourselves into a giant pickle by yelling and losing patience with one another. You are stuck in the mud both physically and metaphorically. You need to find a way to communicate with one another with respect. Leave blame out of the equation. Use your tools, your crystal gifts, and the power of the stones to find common ground. You will then get out of the mud and out of the pickle you find yourselves in. By the way, in case you hadn't noticed, I am not a sweet little Gerkin pickle. I am a big, sour, Kosher pickle!"

For the first time since they had been lectured by this talking pickle, they allowed themselves a little smile. They then took their crystals from their pouches.

"Good, I am happy to see you have decided to use your gifts. I am guessing no one has taught you how to make use of these treasures. Maybe you didn't ask? Life is all about taking responsibility; for yourself, for your actions, and for your interactions with others. First, you need to learn how to quiet your brain *and* your emotions. Learn to communicate and resolve issues inside yourselves before expressing anger, frustration, or even blame outwardly. Once you learn to do this, you can find a new, alternative path for your emotions."

Looks of confusion were apparent as the children looked at the crystals in their hands.

"Listen, learn, and think! I see the confusion on your faces. Please pay close attention as I explain. I will share one way to use your crystals. You will be tested later in life in general about what you learn here today. So, listen, and store this knowledge."

The pickle waited for his words to sink in. Feeling that each child had digested what he was trying to teach them, he continued.

"You can meditate with a stone. One form of meditation is where you take slow, deep breaths, with your eyes closed."

Motioning to them with his eyes, they each began to take slow deep breaths.

"While you are breathing and have your eyes closed, hold your crystal loosely in one hand, or cradled in the palms of two hands together. It's better if you do this while sitting down."

Looking about, they realized they were no longer standing in mud. This opening off the tunnel where the pickle stood, was dry. Taking the cue, they all sat, closed their eyes, and began to breathe slowly.

"Picture your chosen crystal inside your head. Keep breathing. Feel your energy relax as you breathe. Now, you should be able to feel some of the energy the crystal has to offer you. It can be clarity of emotion, of direction, or what you might even say to one another. It could be that your need for anger has left you. Maybe you suddenly feel so at peace inside, that you can voice an opinion to someone without force. Trust what you feel—as long as it is a positive thought pattern. Destructive thoughts should have left your brain while doing this kind of exercise. Keep breathing. Keep clearing your head. Find peace. Find clarity. Find that place inside where everything is possible."

Hearing the calm voice of the pickle, the meditation had helped each child relax.

"When you really feel at peace inside, true peace, you can remain there for a time, and then slowly come back to opening your eyes."

When they eventually opened their eyes, each child was

much calmer. They were relaxed. Their shoulders were no longer tensed up, their anger was gone.

They had regained their sense of normal.

They looked at one another and smiled. The pickle seemed pleased with this reaction.

"Very good! I'm happy with how well you listened to my instructions. Each stone you have in your pouch at this moment is part of the quartz family. All quartz helps bring clarity to you in some manner. Kathy, you had the clear quartz in your hand. I know that particular crystal is a record keeper. Those crystals were programmed by ancient people from Lemuria and Atlantis. These lands are under water today. Those people knew their worlds would cease to exist after a time. While alive, they worked at peaceful existences. They wanted to pass along their knowledge to other societies, and programming their crystals was one way to do just that. When you find clear quartz with raised triangles on the face of one or more tips, you know you are a lucky duck who can tap into ancient knowledge.

"You held onto aventurine, Peter. Aventurine will help you to be clear in your thoughts, as well as how you communicate to others. Think about it like this: sometimes you think in two directions at once. Confusion and frustration come about then. Use aventurine to help you find which thought pattern is most useful for right now, and leave the other one behind."

Facing Gwen, he said, "In much the same way, amethyst helps you to find clarity in how to not overindulge. It can even address how you overindulge in passing blame onto others. I am not judging any one of you, but please realize you each chose to enter this cave. Perhaps Peter gave you the incentive to move forward, but you each entered on your own. Learn to take responsibility for your actions in life and you'll be a happier person for it."

Defensively, Gwen began to open her mouth, and then opted not to fight with the pickle.

"Live life blaming others for where and who you are, and you will be lonely, and sad. Use your stones through meditation and each stone will give you some form of healing as well as information. Being able to tap into this energy will give you tools that will assist you in becoming all that you can be, now and forever. The purpose isn't to make you better than anyone else. It simply helps make a better *you*."

Each child was deep in thought. No one was moving, talking, or even acting confused. Watching how they pondered what he said, the pickle smiled. His work was almost complete.

They were not only calm; they were using the tools given by each of the cave guides. Letting them have a quiet moment, the pickle stood patiently. Once he felt they were ready to shift from their moments of reflection, he made a slight sound. Looking up at him, the children thought he was going to give more information about the crystals.

Instead, he moved to one side of the pyramid with surprising agility. No one could figure out how he moved without legs or feet!

"Pyramids were built many, many years ago by different cultures such as the Egyptians and Mexicans. Without tools or machines like we have today, great boulders were shaped, and carefully moved into position by many people working together."

Motioning with his eyes, he seemed to take in the enormity of the structure. "You can see that by working together great things can be accomplished. Structures like this have survived the perils of time, weather, and earthquakes.

"Now...your stones are tools to help you build an inner tower of strength, like an emotional pyramid. With that inner strength, you are then able to invite others into your world. They may share your beliefs, or not; they may become friends, or not. Being strong inside gives you a sense of calm where it doesn't matter if people share all your convictions, or do what you want them to do. You remove the need to bully someone into believing what you feel is right. Simply, you accept their beliefs, and respect them without the need of force. Disagree of course, and choose a different path than those you do not share values with.

"Use your inner calm to communicate with one another,

share opinions, and then make group decisions on how to move forward. No need to push. No need to feel stuck in the mud. No need to feel someone else has gotten you into a pickle. You all came into the cave looking for an adventure. Use the crystal gifts to find a new direction or path, one that creates peace within, and without. Most important, do not forget to have some fun along the way."

Just then, a door at the base of the pyramid slid open.

The children saw steps inside that led to the top. They caught the pickle smiling and knew it was okay for them to go in.

They followed the steps to the top where there was a great slide down on one of the outer edges of the pyramid.

Jumping onto the slide, they went down shouting with glee. Anger was forgotten and a moment of pure joy took over.

The mud that had been clinging to their clothing fell away. Their clothes were dry again. They moved about freely.

Caught up in the magic of the moment, they kept re-climbing the stairs and sliding down the pyramid over and over again.

Peter kindly tucked Justine between his legs and they went down together.

Even Gwen found she could climb the stairs and join in some physical fun for once.

Sliding down the pyramid, Kathy noticed her feet for the first time since they were all stuck in mud. When they were all together at the base of the pyramid, she said: "I lost a shoe and sock."

"Are they at the top of the slide do you think?" Gwen asked.

"I don't think so. I don't think it matters."

"Well, we ought to look for the shoe, Kathy."

Gwen had instinctively taken over as watch dog and caretaker. She didn't understand why she was being such a mother hen. Maybe turning fourteen should have come with instructions.

"Don't you think we should find Kathy's shoe?" Gwen asked Peter.

He replied: "Kathy is forever losing a shoe. If it's back in the mud, I don't want to go back, do you?"

Before Gwen and Peter could argue the point, Justine pulled out her aventurine. Seeing this, they all followed suit. With eyes closed, they began to take deep breaths.

Calm took over.

The lost shoe and sock became a non-issue.

When they opened their eyes, the pyramid was no longer there. In all the excitement of their fun on the slide, they couldn't remember the last time they had seen the pickle either.

Had their new friend and teacher abandoned them like

all the others in these caves?

Suddenly, they realized they were back in the light of the gray tunnel. The opening where they had found the pickle and the pyramid had closed over.

With a newfound calm in their hearts and minds, they were not in the least bit angry at the pickle for leaving them. Instead, they appreciated how valuable the little time they spent with him was. How special, and how much they had learned.

In the distance, the gray light seemed to shine brighter now.

They moved as one towards it, walking and crawling. As if by magic, there was no longer any mud to impede their journey. Very soon they found themselves standing in front of the opening for the next cave.

Entering the gray cave, they stood together. Their recent past experiences had shown that each time they looked around the perimeter of a cave, someone, or something appeared while their backs were turned.

Choosing to stay focused on the center of the cave this time, and staring straight ahead determined not to miss any magical appearances, they were so very surprised to hear a voice come from over their heads.

"Hello, my friends."

Kathy pointed and yelled out, "A face!"

Slowly they all looked up to the ceiling of the cave.

A very large gray, moon was talking to them.

With eyes, nose, and of course, a mouth, it was translucent with a misty gray glow around its perimeter. Now they understood where the gray light inside the tunnel had come from. They stood looking up at this talking face until they realized they had cricks in their necks.

"If you lay down, you'll find it more comfortable to talk to me. You might be here for some time."

The children did as they were told, and made themselves comfortable looking up from the ground.

"You have come so far, and learned so much on this adventure of yours. Before you leave us here, there are many things you must still learn. This means your adventure is not yet at an end. If you are willing, allow me to teach you about being in tune with lunar—or moon—energy. When you look at the night sky you think of the moon as being white with gray spots on it. I am what is known as a licorice moonstone which is more gray in color.

"My mission is to help you understand how to connect to lunar energy when necessary. You are of an age where some of your thoughts can be scary. Even walking about in these crystal caves, you have each had moments where you thought you would never get home. Am I right?"

Heads were nodding in agreement.

"You have to individually take responsibility for having dark thoughts like that. Dark thoughts can be good if you find a way to turn them around into positive ones. Sometimes this is easy, like turning a frown upside-down to make a smile! Changing your dark thoughts over into positive ones makes not only you, but God happy as well. Maybe you don't believe in God. Maybe you believe in angels. Maybe you believe in Buddha. Perhaps you think there is nothing spiritually beyond what you see on this earth. It's okay to have different beliefs from one another. What matters is how you learn from one another's beliefs. Learning is the key."

Kathy couldn't wait to ask, "Are you God?"

"Are you asking that Kathy because I am high up over your heads, in what comes close to a sky here in the cave?"

"Maybe. I don't know. My mom told me about God, and how he's up in the sky where we can't see him. That when people don't live here anymore, they go up to him."

"Well, Kathy, to answer your interesting question, I will say that, no, I am not God, not in the way you are asking. But I believe we are all part of a god source. By living an enlightened way, and by being tuned into all there is around me, I believe I am a part of God. I am God-like. Maybe that answers your question in a small way."

While Kathy was trying to think about how she could be God-like, the moon face continued.

"Right now, I want you to learn about my stone energy. Even though I am a moonstone, that does not mean you should only work with me after dark. Make use of a licorice moonstone whenever you have need of shining a bright white light into those dark emotional places in your mind. In other words, when you have gloomy thoughts, you can shift them away from being depressing. Move them out of an ugly place into a wondrous place. When you no longer fear what your mind thinks about, you will feel free.

"A while before you came to my cave you each had an emotional melt-down. Some were crying, some were angry. You all were frustrated. That is when you got stuck in the mud. The mud was a metaphor for where you were emotionally. When you get stuck in the mud of negative emotions, you also get stuck in life. It can be a challenge then to find your way out of that negative place. With some help from the enormous pickle, you worked with your crystals and found inner peace. From there you had some fun, shook off those negative thoughts and actions, got back onto your chosen path in life, and now you're here with me. This is proof you shifted that negative energy into positive. Did you feel it was difficult to make that emotional shift?"

Justine and Kathy looked at Gwen and Peter, as if they were the only ones who had a meltdown in the last tunnel.

The overhead head spoke again, this time with a major smile on his face.

"Perhaps you are wondering how it is that I know all this about you four? We here in the cave can, and do, see all who enter. We see your travels in our minds. We have progressed in our spiritual development to a level of enlightenment. That is to say, we each have developed our beliefs as to what is possible inside ourselves. Perhaps you think that because you are unable to hear perfectly, or walk perfectly, or even speak yet beyond the coos of a baby, that you are incapable of doing great things. Deep inside, you know better. It doesn't matter what size you are, or what physical limitations you might have. Each one of you is capable, even at the age you are and the abilities you have right now, to accomplish incredible things!

"Think of how you came to be here. It was no accident you entered the cave this day. There have been other moments when you were all together, walking about the property. We chose this day for you to enter the cave because curiosity and interest in learning new things was evident in all four of you. Lessons you learn in each cavern will be valuable over time. Most important, is for you to remain friends. As companions, you have been marked in the heavens.

"There will be trials and tribulations in your friendships, but you should find your way through those difficulties, and go forward. Friends help you learn. Friends also help you each to remain true to yourself. These four friendships can be like a mirror for your soul. If you are open-minded, you will see things through your friends' eyes that you might not see on your own.

"Friendships help us each to be better all around. So, learn to work together, and remain true to one another as well as yourself. Help each other to find a way out of those dark places we all get into emotionally. Do all this, and you will find your way through life in the best possible way."

The moon face blinked and a compassionate look came over his huge smiling face.

"Since you did work together in order to come into this particular cave, I am giving you each a licorice moonstone for your pouches. It has a carved face so you will always remember this visit with me."

"Is it from the moon?" Kathy asked sincerely and in all innocence.

"No, moonstone does not come from the moon, it is from earth. The name came about because each stone exhibits a sheen of light that reminds people of the moon. Before you ask, this stone is not part of the quartz family. Moonstone is a member of a different group of stones known as feldspar. There are many stone groups and families, just as there are in human societies. Each stone group has specific healing properties.

"Moonstones come in a variety of colors. Each color helps you in slightly different ways. All moonstones help you connect with the energy of the moon, which normally has twelve cycles of being full, generally one cycle for each month. That said, there are times when there are two full moons in a month, and these are referred to as blue moons. Though there are also blue moonstones, what you have in your pouches are licorice moonstones. Use the idea of twelve full moons to shift negative thoughts around to positive ones. Perhaps you recreate your emotions over the course of twelve minutes, twelve hours, or even days. Simply give yourself time to shift from dark thoughts, into light with help from your moonstone.

"Remember to make use of your crystals and stones in life. Take care of them, and they will take care of you."

"How do we take care of our crystals?" Gwen inquired.

"That's an important question!

"When you feel energy in your stones is stagnant, you can shift all that simply. Use warm water and some sea or Kosher salt in a small dish to soak your stones in for however long you feel is necessary to remove that negative energy. It may only be a few minutes, or perhaps an hour. Remove your stone from that water, run clear water, and rinse the stone while reciting, *'Please remove any negative energy from this stone, and allow only white light energy to remain.'* Place the stone on a white paper towel out in the raw sunlight to recharge. You will notice a marked difference in the energy after this procedure.

"There are certain stones this method is not good for, and they are anything organic, opal, emerald, and beads.

"Always discard the salty water down the drain after use as it contains negative energy you do not want in or around your home any longer.

"There are other methods for cleansing stones and crystals, however, this one is simple, and works quite well."

Kathy reached inside her pouch and took hold of the licorice moonstone face.

Running it through her fingers as you would the satin border of a baby blanket, she felt comforted.

The others took hold of their new moonstone and feeling the smoothness in their hands, they began to breathe more slowly.

They smiled at the moon face carved into the stone. When they looked up to compare it to the face overhead, the face was no longer there.

These appearances and disappearances were happening so often now, the children were not fazed.

The gray glow of the cave remained and seemed to gently pulsate.

They knew it was time to move on.

They glanced about the cave expecting a beacon of white light the talking moon face had spoken of.

Surely that would shine a light on which tunnel they should take. Bewilderingly, for a split second, there it was.

It lit up the entrance to one of the tunnels and quickly turned into a soft pink glow.

Without discussion, they walked in that direction. It might not be a white light, but this was the tunnel of their collective, cooperative choice.

Still nervous, they figured the
talking horse was not going to harm them,
but they erred on the side of caution.

Chapter Five:
SELF-LOVE

Everyone noticed this tunnel was different from the others.

In each of the previous tunnels, the light came from the cave up ahead. This tunnel had pink rays that radiated from the glistening stonewalls. No one was quite sure if the stone walls were pink, or if the light itself was that color. They discussed it among themselves. No one disagreed with the other. No one felt upset.

What a contrast!

It was perhaps the calmest they had all been since this adventure began. Everyone actually seemed happy.

Gwen reached out and touched one of the stone walls and said, "It's pretty here."

Pulling out the blowpipe and plastic jar of liquid bubbles he always carried in his back pocket, Peter began to blow bubbles.

Gwen commented on how boys were surprising this way.

"What way?" Peter asked.

"Boys always seem to have more in their pockets than one might think, like your bubbles. It's great!"

The pipe had a few round holes on the surface which made it possible to blow a lot of small bubbles at once. If he just dipped the pipe inside the jar and blew, one larger bubble formed.

Justine delighted in catching and popping them.

Kathy wanted her turn at blowing, so Peter gave the pipe and liquid over to his sister.

Between the glowing pink in this tunnel, and the rainbows shining on each bubble, the children began to laugh and play together.

Gwen blew away the bubbles that floated her way.

They jumped, walked, and played their way up this tunnel surrounded by cascading rainbow bubbles, and a beautiful pink glow. Laughter and giggles helped them forget where they were, at least momentarily.

Then, suddenly, the beautiful music they heard when they first entered the caves struck up again.

They walked towards it. It was coming from a new cave.

Approaching this cave, the sound got stronger, more vibrant.

No one stopped outside this cave when they reached it. They walked inside feeling certain everything would be fine.

There were more tunnel openings around the perimeter of the cave. Even though they were faced once again with making the right tunnel choice, no one seemed to worry.

Maybe it was the pink light.

Maybe it was the bubbles.

Maybe it was the music.

Maybe they were simply getting accustomed to being in

the caves.

This crew of four had momentarily found an emotional center of peace.

Standing together they waited for what they knew would come next: some form of magical appearance.

They were not disappointed.

In the blink of an eye, a horse appeared in the center of the cave.

It was big and brown, with very long eyelashes. It was even taller than Gwen. The size and obvious strength of the horse was a little intimidating. Especially since it didn't stand still, and kept moving its great big hooves about.

Gwen went toward the horse with a great wide smile on her face. The other children tried to grab her clothing as she moved forward, but she pulled away from their attempts to hold her back. Gwen stood right in front of the horse unafraid. She acted as though this was a familiar horse from her barn at home.

After a long minute of exchanging glances with the horse, Gwen turned back to her friends and said, "My mother teaches people how to ride horses. I told you I'm around them all the time. This breed is called a Fresian." Pointing at its feet, she said, "See the longer hair around the hooves? That's one of the tell-tale signs of that breed."

Each child looked more closely at the brown horse, from hooves to head. The horse swished its long, bushy tail up, and around, as if saying, "I'm a noble creature."

Still, only Gwen had the nerve to get so close to the horse. The rest were still concerned the large hooves would stomp them, and do some serious damage.

Suddenly, the horse began to speak. "Hello to you all. I am very happy to see you in my cave today."

All but Gwen took a giant step backward.

Not only was the horse large, and potentially harmful, but now it spoke.

Talking pickles. Talking moons. Now, there was a talking horse to deal with. They shouldn't have been surprised. But they were. Except Gwen.

Gwen apologized to the horse. "I'm sorry my friends are nervous around such a beautiful creature as yourself. Please do not take offense. They really are nice people if you take the time to get to know them."

"That's exactly why you are here, for me to get to know you all. I hope to share some knowledge with you as well. If you can get over the idea I might step on you, we can get started."

Each of the other three children took a baby step forward. Still nervous, they figured the talking horse was not going to harm them, but they erred on the side of caution.

As with their previous encounters, the horse knew them by name.

Motioning with her head about the cave, she said, "This

cave is made of rose quartz. I know you have discovered lots about quartz since your adventure began. This form of quartz is naturally pink in color. If the energy is balanced correctly, there seems to be a glow of pink that resonates outward from the stone. Rose quartz helps you learn how to love yourself, and how to take care of yourself. When you learn these things, you come from a place of inner strength."

Watching their faces, the horse wondered if she ought to continue, or give them a minute to absorb what she had just said.

"Do you mean we are supposed to make our own dinner? Is that taking care of ourselves?" asked Gwen.

Smiling down at her, the horse looked as though this young girl had just said something very charming.

"I do love it when I get asked questions. Thank you, Gwen, for your input. No, I do not mean making dinner for yourselves. Though, at some point you will want to do just that. What I mean today is something so much bigger, and more important than making dinner."

She couldn't express herself with hand gestures, instead the horse moved about the cave to make a stronger point of what she was saying. Her hooves were hard. With each slight movement, the other three children cringed.

"You have a chance at very young ages to learn how to love yourselves. Each of you is different, unique, and special. When you come to appreciate who you are, you will then be able to understand how you might need something or someone to make progress in life. There are moments when you might not like who you are, how you feel, what you have done, or what you said to someone. Moments such as those are what I call the ugly parts. Liking even the ugly parts of yourselves is necessary in order to make headway in life."

Gwen gently protested. "Even the ugly parts? Are you saying I ought to like the fact I have to wear leg braces all the time? They hurt. I can't walk well without them, or with them for that matter. And I can't run like all my friends."

"Yes. You see, when you can find a way to love all the inner and outer parts of yourself, you can then come from a place of strength and balance. When someone comes up to you, like maybe a bully, and tries to bait you into a fight, you would be able to look at that bully and walk away, instead of feeling the need to defend yourself.

"Gwen, think about this. Someone approaches you and says something like, 'Eww, you wear leg braces, how weird is that?' If you know how to love all of yourself, you can look at that person and feel sorry for *them*. In order to feel big themselves, that person needed to verbally knock someone else down. When you are centered and strong inside, with the love of self, you see a bully not as an obstacle, but rather as a sad human being. A bully is someone who feels the need to prove himself all the time. Using other people to make a point of physical strength doesn't make a person strong. In fact, they are really weak. But, there is never a need to point that out to a bully when confronted.

"When your parents or any adult yells at you for doing something wrong, if you really love yourself, you can see this as a moment in time, and not a reflection of your character. All people get frustrated. Often that frustration comes out when someone cannot control a situation. Be centered, and don't take those moments to heart. When you come from a place of inner strength, you can then offer true assistance to others. You won't be helping them for selfish reasons, like the thanks you receive, or for money. Instead, you will be offering help because you know you *can* help, and that that person can *use* your help. Know how to love you first and you are then strong internally, where it counts. This is especially important for you, Gwen, because of the hole that you had in your heart at birth."

"That got sewn up. What do you mean?"

"Holes in the heart can be actual ones, as it was in your case. They can also be a way to describe a lack of emotional development."

The horse could see the four didn't quite understand, so there was need of further explanation.

"Some of what I am telling you, you won't comprehend

today. But you will recall it when the time is right later in your life. Some of what I am saying is what you will need more immediately to finish your journey while here in the cave."

She had their attention.

All children were focused and listening.

"When you have a hole in your heart, either for real or due to emotions, you are not all you can and ought to be as a person. A physical hole in your heart means you need medical attention to fix it. If you have an emotional hole in your heart, there might be times when you need to talk to someone older and wiser, or even a special therapist. These people will hopefully listen, and make possible suggestions that will be helpful to heal your heart. If you are trying to heal your emotional heart on your own, please remember that forgiveness is key to all in life. Forgiving yourself, as well as others, will allow your heart to blossom into its fullest potential."

Gwen nodded her head in understanding.

The horse looked away from her and over at the younger children in the group. They were starting to comprehend what the horse had been saying as well. She continued.

"Each one of you is wonderful, special, and full of potential. Not only in what you might accomplish in this life, but also because of how you deal with the people around you. It's always good to listen to what others say to you."

The young adventurers had clearly taken in what the horse had been saying.

Now each child had a bit of an inner glow about them, kind of like the rock walls of the tunnel and cave they were in now.

It was special in this cave. No one wanted to leave. They had been afraid of the horse, and her strength, but they now knew she was no bully, and had no intent to cause them any harm.

Their pouches felt heavier. Reaching into them simultaneously, they each found a brilliant, light pink stone. Smiles along with sighs came from each one, and a sense of calm filled the cave.

Certain the horse would disappear about now, each child felt it was time to begin looking at their choices to move forward when the horse spoke again.

"There are two more things I'd like to share with you each today. They come under the heading of loving the ugly parts I've already mentioned."

Each child grimaced while preparing for what might come next.

"When you lose your temper, or when you act like a bully, or when you act like you know it all, it is vital to love that part of yourself. No one is perfect. No one gets through life without losing his or her temper. At some point, you will think you know everything there is to know about whatever someone else is saying. These are the parts inside that we consider ugly, yet they're human. It's important to forgive those parts of yourself, and send love to your inner self because forgiveness of yourself and others is powerful. When you do not find forgiveness for yourself and others, you block all kinds of good that is already yours, and can come to you with ease."

The atmosphere had become rather serious.

The horse sensed the children needed something uplifting. She began to vibrate her lips, like a human would do to create the sound of raspberries. They giggled. Giggles gave way to outright laughter. Kathy buckled over with laughter. Gripping her stomach, she rolled about on the cave floor. When she got a handle on herself, Kathy asked, "Pretty pink please, do more!"

Swishing of the tail and more raspberry noises let them release some of their pent-up energy. Soon they lovingly mocked the horse, and made raspberry sounds as well.

Feeling it was time to get back to business again, the horse put her right hoof forward, and stomped it on the ground a few times, as if she was digging a hole. The children stopped laughing and paid attention.

"The final point I need to cover with you today is about envy. Envy happens when you are jealous of what someone else has, or who someone else is, and you feel it ought to be you instead. Jealousy and envy block everything good in life. These are especially unhealthy ugly parts of yourselves you need to pay attention to."

Scrunched faces let the horse know they did not completely understand what she was saying.

"Let me tell you a story. When I was young, like you, I felt sad that another horse got so much attention. That horse got more pats, and compliments than I had ever received. I felt these words and pats ought to be coming my way. That was jealousy. The other horse had no idea I felt this way. It was used to getting attention, and didn't know anything different. One day I thought about what I could do to make that horse lose favor with all the people who normally paid him attention. Filled with jealousy, I wanted to take my envy out on that horse. Do you see what I am saying?"

They all nodded.

"Okay, well, I was lucky at that moment. An older horse I lived next to saw my attitude shift from friendly to jealousy and envy. It was written all over me by the way I stood, and looked at everyone, especially when I looked at that other horse. This elder horse took me to one side and suggested I shift my thinking. After all, that other horse didn't know anything different. It wasn't the horse's fault everyone fawned all over him. The people who paid attention actually did that horse a great disservice. That horse grew up to feel it was his right to be important all the time, like he ought to get special attention forever. On the other hand, I grew up knowing there are good moments, and not so good moments in life. Sometimes you get accolades for what you do, how you look, or simply for being in the right place at the right time. When you feel the need to knock someone else down for what they have or are, your path and energy are confused, and blocked. Energy that could come your way will pass you by.

"I was fortunate to have that older and wiser horse give me advice, along with a piece of rose quartz. Learn this really big lesson of how to love all the parts of yourself, inside and out, and you will find life easier as you grow up. When you really love even the ugly parts, you can forgive your ugly blip moments, and find inner peace."

The horse felt the children needed to absorb what she had been telling them and remained quiet for a few minutes. Then she delivered her final message.

"Everyone has done well today. You listened to what I said, and I hope, have understood it all. Some will remember more than others. Being of different ages is a good thing. Each member of you will remember differently, and can then share with the others later on. When you share, new comprehension can be realized and carried forward. When you invite others to come into your world with open hearts, anything is possible. Most important, do remember to laugh at yourselves. Laughter helps to keep your energy centered, light, and loving. This is a lot to ask, but all of what I say will bring you great happiness in the years to come."

In the blink of an eye again, the horse was gone.

They all shrugged their shoulders, as if to say, "Oh well."

They had all been so engrossed in the horse, and what she was saying, they hadn't realized the music they heard coming into the cavern had stopped. It had now started again and seemed to be coming from one particular tunnel that was now lit up with an orange light.

It felt warm, inviting, and not threatening, so they began to walk towards it when Justine gurgled aloud.

*There were disembodied blue eyes floating around
the perimeter of the scallop, sort of in the recess part of the
shell curves, yet floating above them.*

Chapter Six:
WEALTH

Everyone stopped and looked at Justine.

"Justine doesn't seem to want us to go into this tunnel," said Gwen.

"We always enter a tunnel because color shines from it as we walk up to it," said Peter.

Doubt now filled them all. They stood frozen with uncertainty.

It was Justine who moved first. The smallest of the group suddenly started walking towards one of the tunnels to the right of the one with the orange light. They all followed her ready to pull her back from any danger she might be getting into.

A new color presented itself as Justine closed in on it. The light was a blue-gray tone.

Panic came over them like a blanket. The peace they experienced in this pink cave drained out of them. No one grabbed a pouch for the crystal-powered calm and clarity of thinking they needed right now. Realization that they had chosen each tunnel because a color had presented itself was sinking into the deep recesses of Gwen and Peter's minds.

Was it possible that each tunnel had a light to show, but they had only seen one light first, so it felt correct to go there? If that were the case, then perhaps each choice made thus far actually led them deeper into the cave than they had hoped. Maybe it meant they could have been out of the cave already if they had chosen differently.

Justine walked on.

Peter and Gwen grabbed hold of her arms to stop her. Peter asked no one in particular, "Why towards the blue-gray wight?"

"Because it's the right way to go."

They instantly let go of Justine's arms as if they were on fire and would burn them. The shock of hearing the youngest member speak left them wide-eyed and speechless themselves. She spoke in such a clear voice you would think she had been much older.

Did they really hear her speak?

If so, what strange magic was this?

So far today, if in fact it still *was* today, a giraffe, the moon, and a horse had all talked to them. (Not to mention the pickle!)

Surely all that was magic?

On some odd level the children had grown to not only expect, but to also accept these weird happenings. Now, the clear audible voice of their youngest member, only twelve months old, had completely thrown them.

Her words were loud and clear.

"Come on. This is the way."

Justine headed into the blue-gray tunnel.

Kathy went in after her.

The other two companions followed—once they could get their legs to move!

Justine was now moving forward with such certainty the other three felt it must be the correct way to go. If it wasn't, they wouldn't be any more lost than they were now.

Still, questions ran rampant in the older children's minds. The peace they had experienced was gone; fear took its place.

Fear for what could possibly come next.

Fear of never getting out of the cave.

Fear of maybe meeting up with some form of black magic!

Each fear came into their heads too quickly to process, that is, if they were even capable of processing what was happening.

Peter spoke first. His voice cracked with nervousness. "Justine, what makes you so sure we are going in the wight direction? I mean, you haven't given any verbal input on choices until now. So how come we should twust this choice?"

Gwen added: "Justine, I am not sure we actually heard you say this was the way. Maybe we *thought* we heard you say this was the tunnel to choose." Her own voice was shaking.

You could have cut the anxiety in the air with a knife. Everyone except Justine stopped.

Without turning around, Justine responded gruffly.

"This *is* the way to go. Come with me or not, it's up to you!"

Yup, they had heard her speak.

That was abundantly clear now.

Whether it was magic, or a strange phenomenon found only in this cave, no one knew, but onward they walked.

This tunnel was a short one. When the opening to the next cave came upon them, Gwen reached out for Justine to stop her.

"Wait Justine. Let's look inside first. Let's make sure it's safe before entering."

"I already know it's safe. Come or don't come. I've been talking to the cave, so I know to go ahead."

Not only was she talking, but her speech was clear and confident. Had she always been able to speak and had chosen this moment to show the others what she was capable of? How could she already be talking to someone or something inside the next cave? They hadn't gotten beyond the fact that she was using words, let alone speaking to someone outside their range of eyesight.

This was exactly what they were afraid of: Black Magic!

Let's face it, if they didn't understand how things kept appearing and then disappearing, how could they explain Justine talking to them? And now, talking to the cave?

Shaking off the horrible thought that something might happen to Justine on their watch, they hurried after her as she walked into the cave. Kathy followed quietly.

Inside the new cavern, the light had changed.

It was now a blue-black tone, instead of the gray-blue color they had experienced in the tunnel. Black is a color you would see when gloom was about to descend, yet in here it was quite inviting.

Then a sudden flash of bright pink light took their breath away.

Before they had recovered, the pink color faded back to black, like when the brilliant color of a firework in the sky fades silently and slowly away.

Another dramatic flash of light, this time, blue to black.

When the blinding white flash happened, they had to cover their eyes to shut out the sudden brightness. After that died down, it was back to black again.

They removed their hands from their eyes and looked up to see a very large scallop in the center of the cave.

There were disembodied blue eyes floating around the perimeter of the scallop, sort of in the recess parts of the shell curves, yet floating above them.

Not surprisingly given their experiences so far, the scallop began to speak.

It's double layer of shell moved slightly in and out as it spoke, as if there was a heart beating inside.

What caught them all completely off guard was that the voice of the scallop sounded just like Justine's. The voice they had heard in the tunnel. Looking back and forth between the scallop and Justine, everyone had giant question marks on their faces.

How could this be happening?

"I see your confused faces," said the giant scallop. "Let me explain what is going on. Justine and I have been communicating since before you entered my tunnel. She has a lot to say, if you listen. I gave her the ability to speak. Once you become accustomed to her talking, you will then *hear* what she has to say."

The children were mesmerized.

The scallop continued. "Justine and I are going to speak to you. Some of the time, it will be both our opinions you hear."

Their minds were jumbled, and they were still trying to process Justine speaking and being in communication with a scallop!

"You have not even considered the fact that Justine might have an opinion as to what tunnel you chose to walk into."

Noses crinkled up and Gwen and Peter felt guilty.

In fact, they had only stopped to ask what Justine thought once. In their eyes, Justine was a cute baby that they had to keep an eye on while their parents enjoyed visiting. Concentrating solely on Justine, Peter and Gwen had momentarily stopped thinking about Kathy in all this.

Now it was her turn to feel a bit indignant.

"I thought Justine would let us know somehow if she disagreed, but she didn't say anything, so I thought she was okay with each tunnel we took."

"You are quite right, Kathy," the scallop said. "If she objected strongly, she would have made herself known in some manner. While on this adventure it's important to take *everyone* into consideration. There have already been times where no one wanted to listen to one another. However, hearing what one of your friends has to say is always important, even if they cannot use words yet. Both Justine and I want you to consider that she counts as much as you all do."

While the children were processing what had just been said, the scallop jiggled about in place as if it was shaking something, or some idea off its shells. Its eyes were moving about in all directions at once.

"We need to stress the point that you each have a voice. Even when you do not understand what someone is saying, you need to listen. Justine may have important suggestions if you make an effort to ask, and then pay attention to her tone and physical movements. In case you haven't noticed, her sparkling eyes speak volumes. But you must pay attention. Listening to others through expression, not just talking, gives you a broader spectrum of understanding as well."

Justine reverted to coos and gurgles that only the scallop understood.

"You're quite right Justine. I will tell them."

Turning its attention back to the other three children, the scallop began to explain.

"Before each of you were born, you decided to come to earth, and join the family you have now. Even babies born to parents who are unable to keep them choose their birth parents. You learn specific things from the home you choose. Justine is the only one of you four that is still in her *forgetting* phase. The *forgetting* phase is why you cannot speak with the use of words when you are born.

"God wants you to *forget* what Heaven is like, so you can live your life without the desire to return to Heaven before your time here is finished. You see, right now Justine can remember Heaven and all the friends she left behind there. Those souls hope she will do well while here on earth. They hope her experience is educational, full of love, understanding, and fun. She's excited to be here with all of you on this learning adventure in the crystal caves.

"Though she is the youngest of your group, Justine will remember the most of this experience in the years to come. She will write about your adventure so that others can share with their children what happened. Justine will enlighten you in later years about Heaven and her recollections. You see, she will be one of the chosen ones who does recall what Heaven is like after the forgetting phase. It's no accident she looks like a fairy."

Gwen stiffened up as she tried to wrap her brain around what she just heard.

"Yes, Gwen, I read your mind when you recognized the fairy-like qualities in Justine's features. That thought happened before you even entered the cave today. Fairies, their world, and all they touch can only be described as magical! Her recollection of the cave experience will bring you all visually and emotionally back here as you age. You'll smile over your tribulations, and be amazed at your own tenacity to go forward. All that will come to you much later in life. What I'd like you to understand now is, that communication is available to all members of your group. We here in the cave do not have difficulties understanding any one of you, yet none of you have felt it was necessary to *work* at communicating with Justine."

Noticing the confused looks on their faces, the scallop took a different tack. "Do you have animals at home as pets?"

Heads nodded yes.

"Okay then, when your animals talk, they do not use words like you and I do, right? Yet you can tell what they are trying to say by body language, as well as the sounds they make. Sometimes they even travel to where it is they want you to pay attention, like their food dish, or water bowl."

The children were on board now, understanding the scallop's point. They knew what was coming next.

"Justine is trying to tell you things with her body language, facial expressions, as well as the sounds she makes. So, you ought to be able to include Justine in your decision making, not just while here in the cave, but onward once you return home."

"*Ahh*" sounds come from all as they wrapped their brains around this latest explanation.

"Now," continued the scallop, "you're here in the crystal caves. And though stones do not speak out loud to you, like Justine, they have loads to tell you when you work with them properly. That is true of pearls as well. While you are here in my cave, I would like to tell you about pearls and share the energy that a few different colored pearls give off.

"First, let me tell you how pearls are formed. Pearls are organic by nature, not like the stones you have been discovering that come out of the ground. Pearls grow inside mollusks in the ocean, and even in fresh water, too. A substance called nacre forms most pearls. Nacre to mollusks is like saliva to humans. It will coat a grain of sand, or almost any other foreign thing that aggravates the soft muscle inside the mollusk shell. Pearl essence is another name for nacre. Nacre coats, and then recoats that thing that is aggravating the inner muscle, layer upon layer until a pearl is formed. The bigger the pearl often means the more layers of nacre on them. Generally, pearls are thought to come from such mollusks as oysters, clams, or quahogs. Because I can also grow pearls, though infrequently, I have chosen to be part of your lessons while you are here."

The children were paying close attention to the scallop.

"White pearls are the most prevalent color of pearls today, and that color pearl brings a pure balance to feminine energy. You can use white pearls when you are feeling out of sorts emotionally. Before Peter tries to tell us he is not a girl, let me say that everyone has some feminine and some masculine energy inside."

Peter made a funny grimace and the others smiled at him.

"Next is the pink pearl. There are many pearls that have a white base, and then a bit of a pink cast to them. I'm talking about a real pink tone pearl. Pink pearls help you find inner comfort and self-acceptance creating a balance within your feminine energy. You can call this self-love if you want. Many stones and organic matter overlap in what they can bring your way energetically.

"When you're having difficulty grasping how to bring self-love into your world, use the rose quartz you've just discovered. If you know you're working on self-love, but feel out of sync with it, use pink pearls to create a new balance. Better still, use both rose quartz with pink pearls to bring clarity and balance to self-love.

"There are many times throughout life when people criticize you for one reason or another. It can be challenging not to take it personally. If you work with the energy found in pink pearls, you can find a way back into balance with accepting who you are: the good and the not-so-good."

Nods all around encouraged the shell to move on.

"Blue pearls can be either light blue, or have a bit of a gray tone in the blue, and they help you understand inside what ought to be said out loud. Be balanced inside, and then what comes out of your mouth can be exactly what you want people to hear. Sometimes you get caught up in the emotion of a moment. When that happens, it's difficult to explain what you would like to come out of the situation. Use the blue pearl to find what it is you really want to say, and then say it. You will come from a place of inner peace, with direction and purpose, rather than full of emotion."

The children were now deep in thought.

"Black pearls are also important. They show you how wealthy you are, even if you do not have money in your pocket. They give you a wealth of understanding. They help you grasp what to work on today, and then work on the next item of priority afterwards. When you know which items to pay attention to, you help your inner self find daily balance. With daily balance, you feel centered, and on some level, full. Feeling full is also a form of wealth."

Anticipating new additions to their golden pouches, the children looked inside.

Sure enough, there were four different colored pearls.

The children rolled the beautiful treasures around in their hands.

Their smaller shape felt different to all the other stones, and yes, they made the children feel balanced, and somehow, wealthy.

"What we give to you in the form of information while you are each here in the caves, will weave in and out of your minds throughout your lives yet to come. No one expects you to remember everything we say, all at once. You will not be tested on any of this information before you leave. Not on paper that is. How impatient you are with one another, or experience frustration from not knowing what you have done by coming into the caves, are examples of how you are being tested.

"As an example, Peter, you led the pack coming into the cave as an adventure. Later, you felt guilty for leading everyone inside, which showed up in you as impatience. Instead of communicating what you felt with words, or how sorry you were for bringing everyone into possible danger, you became testy towards your friends.

"Gwen, you thought that by being the eldest you had the

responsibility of taking care of everyone. You showed that with a bossy attitude that no one felt was fair. Fear of being cross-examined by all parents when you exit the cave and return home had your emotions in high gear. Thoughts of standing up to that scrutiny has you trying to lead everyone to the best of your abilities. Again, I will say, that if *you* spoke about your inner feelings, everyone would have understood exactly what your worries were. They would then perhaps show some support, so you wouldn't have to continue to feel like such a caretaker."

Gwen and Peter were not particularly pleased at hearing their faults described by this scallop.

Kathy was next.

"Kathy, you have been very fortunate. You are young enough not to have taken on a specific role here today. Simply put, you were able to be you at any given moment. That is something that your elders have somewhat forgotten how to do, and some of why they have fought with one another. Living by being true to yourself is a good thing. Others can see, and desire that ability, and even choose to adopt to your way of being.

"Justine however, has had the biggest job in these caves, because she has to communicate in odd ways to get everyone's attention.

"As you grow older, you take on jobs, both in a work mode, as well as when you interact with other people.

Interacting with others can be some of the most challenging things you do in life, and yet it can also be the most rewarding. You won't ever feel alone if you work *with others* throughout life. Sharing takes courage. Sharing deepens your friendships more than you can ever imagine. Trust that your friends, your true friends, want only the best for you, and you begin to see the light inside yourself. Use the black pearls that are now in your pouches to know that in your heart, you have a wealth of spirit.

"Learn what you have inside on all levels. By that I mean spiritually, emotionally, mentally, artistically, creatively, and even mechanically. Working with your inner humor is also important, like when you all had fun with the bubbles. Don't let what happens outside yourself run you, or work against you. Master your fears and you can go far. Let them run you, and it will be your ruin. Each time you feel frustrated, you sink into the emotion of despair. Think about the word despair. Break it down into two words, first is *des...* that means to separate, and *pair*, which means to match things up. When you despair over anything, you are separating what is good and strong within. When you pair up both with your inner self and your friends, you become stronger and more whole in spirit. Your friendships are enough wealth to last a lifetime, and beyond. They give you the strength to be more powerful than you are alone.

"You can live and exist almost alone in life, but won't it be so much richer if you share yourself and your experiences with others?

"Learning to share while here in the caves can be done easily when you include Justine. She is not a baby who is slowing you down. Because she still remembers Heaven, she can add insight to this trip—giving you clarity on why you are traveling the path you are on.

"It's important you learn, each and every day how to be a better you. Learn to be comfortable alone, and then learn how to understand other's opinions, whether you agree with them or not. In this way, you expand not only your consciousness, but your world as well. The whole world becomes your home.

"Think of the world like a shell, that is capable of being open or closed. Both hermit crabs and scallops have shell homes. A hermit crab closes off most of its body inside its shell. I open my doors in order to learn, eat, and grow! How open or closed will your world be? The choice is yours, my friends."

The scallop's final words echoed around and around the vast interior of the cavern.

How open or closed will your world be?
How open or closed will your world be?
How open or closed will your world be?
The choice is yours, my friends.

The choice is yours, my friends.
The choice is yours, is yours, is yours.
And then...

*"Hello, hello. Welcome, welcome.
I've been expecting your arrival."*

Chapter Seven:
STRUGGLE

The scallop shell disappeared.

Gone.

Vanished.

It was all too much. No one spoke for a good length of time. How could they? They were confused.

Unsure of the meaning of everything the scallop had told them, and given it was no longer here to explain things to them again, they replayed the conversations in their minds to see if the lessons the scallop had imparted would become clearer.

Justine turned towards the group and made a gurgling sound.

That reminded them.

The point the scallop made about communicating with Justine had been clear enough. They needed to include her while deciding what to do next, and what was best for the whole group.

They all squatted on the ground at Justine's side. While at Justine's eye level, they began to discuss the lessons the scallop had given them and what they should do.

Along with talking to each other, they used a kind of sign language to express things, like how they were hungry, needed food, and especially a drink in the hope that Justine would be able to understand the sign language and follow along.

They were making a special effort to include her and the scallop would have been proud of that.

So engrossed in signing, they missed an important shift inside the cave.

"Look! Look at the light!" exclaimed Kathy.

It was white. But not the same white as before. It was somehow dense. More like the white of a bedsheet hanging on a clothesline in the sun rather than the soft glow from a lightbulb.

Looking around, they noticed one tunnel seemed to shine with more light than the others.

Slowly, they stood and faced that tunnel.

Walking towards it, they stopped and looked at Justine, as if to ask if she agreed. A gurgling coo told them she did, and unified, they headed into the tunnel and their next experience.

When they were deep inside this tunnel, the air became heavy, and filled with moisture. As if a literal cloud was hanging over their heads.

"I don't understand this, the air is heavy, like we're in fog, yet different," said Gwen.

They then stopped in their tracks. A few minutes ago, they had been desperate for a drink, but now, they were no longer thirsty.

"I just got a drink from the sky," said Kathy.

"You know, I did, too," said Gwen.

Justine was smacking her lips in agreement. It was like the cave had tended to their need. The girls looked at Peter.

"What? What are you all wooking at?" He sounded impatient.

"Did you get a drink from the sky too, Peter?" Kathy asked nicely trying to head off her brother's mood.

"Of course not. Ridiculous. Silly girl," said Peter with unnecessary harshness in his voice.

Concerned how quickly Peter's attitude had changed, Gwen also tried to set things right. "You know Peter, we are simply asking if you're thirsty, or if you feel like you had a drink as well? No one is trying to put you on the spot here."

"You're all wooking at me funny. I'm out-numbered by girls. It's not fair. There ought to be another boy in here I could tawk to."

"You've spoken to quite a few guys in here, Peter."

He squinted at Gwen, and his eyes suggested he was silently screaming, *"I'm angry!"*

Gwen ignored Peter's dagger stares.

"Well you have!" she said calmly but firmly. "You spoke with that guy in the white dress in the first cave. You talked to the pirate. The pickle was a guy, wouldn't you say? You talked to him, too. Honestly, you've spoken to almost everyone we've met in these caves. Why are you suddenly mad again? Is this a five-year-old mad, or are you really angry about something?"

Eyes flaring, he retaliated. "Five-year-old mad! What's that supposed to mean?"

Taking a breath, Gwen tried a different tack. In the most calm voice she could muster, she said. "Sometimes, Peter, you get frustrated for what seems to me like no reason. If I remember correctly, when I was five-ish, I was like that, too. Honestly, I even get like that now, even though I'm fourteen. It's not bad exactly, it's just not easy for the people around you. Let's face it. We can't do anything about the fact that you came in here with three girls. That's just what happened. My suggestion is to deal with it."

Peter's face scrunched. His anger was building. Seeing that, Kathy said, "Peter, be nice. Please."

He stomped his feet, kicked at the dirt, and began to take off on his own. He was almost gone into the whiteness when Gwen yelled out, "Peter, *stop!*"

Whenever Peter got yelled at he would, in fact, pay attention. He now stopped, and with hands defiantly on his hips, listened to Gwen.

"Whatever you do, do not leave the group Peter."

A moment of silence came over them. Crisis averted. Gwen spoke again. Her voice was a bit shaky after this latest outburst.

"You know, I'm a bit turned around suddenly. Peter, are you sure the direction you were about to walk in is the one we began to travel in this tunnel?"

The worry in Gwen's voice snapped Peter out of his funk. He sensed her fear and wanted to help. He was honest with her though. "I'm not sure whether it was this way or not."

Kathy had been facing Justine through all this. Turning back towards Gwen and Peter, her smile was so big her cheek dimple stood proud. The direction Justine was facing when they stopped had saved the day again. Kathy pointed and exclaimed, "It's that way."

She was so confident and happy, they were all caught up in her certainty, and began to fall in behind her lead. If she had it wrong, then they would all be wrong. At least they would be together.

Gwen couldn't let this whole thing with Peter go any further. This day in the caves was hard enough without his mood swings.

At fourteen, some of her stubborn personality was showing. She turned back towards him and lifted her right hand. Forming a "V" shape with her index and middle finger, she moved the fingers from in front of her eyes, and then pointed them at Peter's. Without words, she was telling him she had her eyes on him.

Peter knew she meant it, and rather than disgruntle her

further, he felt he ought to buck up and not be so angry. Although he didn't like being threatened, he gave in to it.

Everyone walked, deep in thought. They were still trying to process all they heard back in the scallop cave.

How could a black pearl teach them about wealth?

The shell spoke of the wealth of spirit, and how each member of this group had it, or they would not have entered the cave.

What was wealth anyway?

Even at young ages they knew money had power, but beyond buying items, what did wealth mean?

How else could wealth play into their lives?

Didn't the shell say that wealth was all around, always, that knowledge was wealth, too, and that friendships were a type of wealth? They knew one another because their parents were friends.

Would they have ever met if their parents didn't know one another? If they hadn't met, then they wouldn't be here in the cave together.

Even though these four companions didn't choose one another in life, they *were* together, and friends on some level.

Before they knew it, the next cave entrance was upon them.

Stopping just shy of the entrance, the weary travelers peeked inside.

What they saw caught them completely off guard.

So far, each cave they had visited had been clean and empty.

The floor of this cave was littered with off-white objects of all different shapes and sizes.

One especially large object lay on its side in the front. It was smooth. The wide end was roundish and then it tapered, and became narrow at the other end.

Standing upright on top of this object was a little gray mouse. He had on a top hat, and in one hand, a black cane with a white grip. Tipping his hat with his free hand, he began to speak.

"Hello, hello. Welcome, welcome. I've been expecting your arrival. Please, do come into my humble home."

The fact the mouse spoke didn't come as a surprise to anyone. Animals talking was becoming the norm in here!

The mouse definitely had a masculine voice. Gwen glanced at Peter as if to say, *"See, another guy you can talk to..."*

Looking around the cave floor, no one felt they could enter given it was so littered with all these whitish objects.

Where would they stand? There wasn't even room to sit on the ground.

Realizing their hesitance, the mouse spoke up.

"Please, do come forward. Come in. Come in and find a seat. Anywhere will do. Come, come, don't be shy."

Magically, a path opened up before them as the smooth

off-white objects rearranged themselves into tidy bench-like seating. Seating that was a perfect height for everyone.

At the invitation of the mouse, they stepped forward.

Instead of taking a seat, Kathy ran over to the mouse. She stood taller than him even though he was standing on his platform. They were almost nose-to-nose.

Her dimple now stood out like her smile, and her eyes were dancing with delight. It was as though she had known the mouse forever. But there was no way she *could* know this little creature…was there?

They sat waiting to see what would come next.

Someone or something magically appeared in each cave and had shared a story, information, or both with them. Before they left each cave, they received gifts. They had heard about things they knew nothing about before. They saw things they had never seen before.

"Ah, I see you are all wondering about all kinds of things."

Everyone looked surprised when the mouse said this. How could he know what they were thinking?

"Yes. Yes, I can read your minds. The voice in Kathy's mind is the strongest, not just because she is standing in front of me, but because she feels she knows me somehow."

Kathy nodded. She definitely felt a connection. It made her bold enough to ask, "What's that in your hand?"

"It's a baton carved out of a wood called ebony, and tipped with ivory," replied the mouse proudly. "Ebony is a rare, naturally black colored wood that contrasts nicely with bone and ivory colors. This is a magical baton with the power to move around the treasures on the floor of my cave when I point it at them. Some of the elephants that left their tusks here for me to keep guard over, bestowed it upon me as a gift. You see, when an elephant has an inkling it is about to die, it comes to this cave to find peace, knowing I will watch over its treasured ivory tusks.

"Over the course of time, elephants have been killed by people not caring about the grandness of this magnificent pachyderm. Once they kill the elephant, they take the long tusks and sell the ivory on what's called the black market. That's a place where people don't care about where the ivory or any other ill-gotten items came from. They just want to know who will pay a high price for it. You see, you shouldn't have ivory from an elephant. Hey, you wouldn't want to be hunted for your teeth, now would you?"

Grabbing their mouths with their hands, everyone nodded in unison about the thought of having their teeth pulled and harvested by some weird hunter.

Kathy was searching the inside of her mouth with her tongue to make sure her teeth were all still where they belonged.

"Does the tooth fairy bring our teeth here, like the

elephant brings its tusks?" she asked the mouse.

"No, the tooth fairy does not come here with *your* teeth. And with all due respect, your teeth are not quite as valuable as the ivory or the special bones I stand guard over."

Gwen wrinkled up her nose. "Bones! Do you mean we might be sitting on a bone from something?"

"Yes."

"Gross!" Gwen pulled herself to her feet and made quite a face of disgust.

"Let me say, you need strong bones to keep you upright."

"I know about that," Gwen said, still sounding a bit disgusted. "My parents told me when I was growing my bones were not strong enough to support me. But I've learned how to walk, and get around with the help of my braces."

Standing sideways now so everyone could easily see her leg braces, all nodded in acknowledgement and agreement.

"So, this effort on your behalf to get your legs stronger has been a challenge for you?" asked the mouse.

"Yes."

"Lucky you! Lucky you!"

What could the mouse possibly mean by this last remark? The children didn't need to ask for an explanation.

"You have learned a valuable lesson with your struggle to walk, Gwen. That lesson was all about hardship, both physical as well as emotional. You have learned how to use the tools at your disposal in order to be able to walk and get around as normally as possible. Your 'normal' might not be the same 'normal' as for others. However, by taking this hardship, and turning it into something that works for you, you are the winner of that lesson."

Although his speech was directed to Gwen, the mouse wanted to make sure all the children understood what he was telling them. Gwen sat back down as he continued.

"This applies to each of you. If you are knocked down by life emotionally, or physically, you can choose to sit and feel sorry for yourself, or you can learn from what life has presented to you. Gwen learned from her experiences. Those braces help her, and she knows it. They have become an accessory for her like any pair of shoes might be to the rest of you. Her hardship has been turned around. That is why I said to her, *lucky you.*

"Hold ivory or bone in your hands and you will sense its healing power. When you feel bombarded by life, and all the difficulties that present themselves to you, ivory or bone can help you move on from that struggle, work your way through difficult moments, find inner strength, or gain strength from those around you. Perhaps you are *supposed* to discover some form of lesson and learn it as Gwen did, so that you can move on in a new direction. That's part of life on this planet. There will always be hardships and lessons to be learned. As long as you are alive, you will be in school."

Gwen and Peter let out a moan at the sound of "school."

Smiling over at them, the mouse understood their response. "I mean the School of Life, where you will always have the opportunity to learn. What is important in life is to not give up on your personal growth. Remember those autumn leaves you were kicking around before you entered the caves? In nature, the trees that drop their leaves in the fall, grow new, strong ones come spring. People are like that, too. Sometimes, we have to discard things from our lives, take a step back, before we can find new growth. The healing power of ivory or bone will help you step back and find inner strength again. You can then move forward with renewed energy."

The mention of the autumn leaves made the children more homesick than ever. They looked down at their feet, and suddenly the idea of confronting snakes as they kicked among the leaves didn't seem so bad after all. At least they would have been outside in the freedom of the backyard. Peter looked up when he heard the mouse say his name.

"Peter, occasionally you have struggles with words, especially when your hearing aids are not in. Children you play with do not understand what it is like to hear differently. That is one struggle you deal with daily. This is where holding bone will be a comfort. It won't help you to hear better, or to help Gwen walk without braces. Instead, it'll help you on an emotional level. Hold onto bone during times of great stress to find inner peace. Once you discover that inner peace, you can find a new pathway to express yourself. You all now have a piece of bone to assist your future endeavors."

Sure enough, their pouches were now heavier by one piece of bone each.

"Speaking of pathways," said the mouse. "Do you now see the tunnel you must follow from here today?"

Gwen spoke up. "I hope it's this tunnel here to my left."

She pointed to an opening that had appeared out of nowhere.

"What tunnel you choose is up to you all. But before you leave my company, I would like to share a little more about how bone and ivory have been used over the course of time."

They were all feeling comfortable with the mouse and no one seemed in a hurry to move. Gwen was happy to be sitting—it helped rest her legs since they had been standing and walking so much today.

"Many, many years ago," the mouse continued. "The world maps looked very different from today. Animals that no longer exist roamed land masses that covered almost the entire planet. Because so many of those continents shifted and are now divided by sea, those same animals will never meet up again. Over time, my family kept secrets for each of those animals. Woolly mammoths, dinosaurs, and more recently, elephants and camels to name just a few, have stopped here to share their stories, adventures, and even their sorrows. My family has passed this information down from generation to generation to keep a record. You could say my family history is one of being record keepers."

The children were loving this. Woolly mammoths in this very cave! Peter moved closer to the mouse so he didn't miss hearing anything.

"We have met whales here, too. They came to visit long ago when they were being hunted. Since we are discussing ivory and bone, I'd like to talk about whale teeth. When a whale gives up a tooth in friendship, it can become many things. In ancient times, stories were scratched on to it. Symbols, words, numbers, and even pictures. Those scratches would then be dyed with tea stains so the designs would stand out. Today, those pieces are called scrimshaw.

"There was a time when ancient mariners hunted whales. They made lamp oil and perfume from their fat. Teeth were taken from these whales by the ship's crew and some began to make the scrimshaw pieces I have described. The problem is, these teeth were not given by choice from a whale."

"That's so sad," Kathy exclaimed.

"This is a good time to mention that these ancient

mariners didn't know they were doing anything wrong. In a way, they were not to blame. For them it was a way to make a living. At least some of those whalers opted to save the teeth of these magnificent creatures and create artwork on them. Once done with their artwork, they presented these cherished items to their loved ones. Some even sold pieces to create additional income."

Kathy began to jump up and down. No one understood why.

"I know about this," she said. "My grandma told me about a man who used to make scrimshaw. It was Milton."

The mouse nodded his head.

"Yes, Kathy, you're correct. Milton Delano was very well known for his scrimshaw. How wonderful of you to remember that name."

"Grandma has a pin, and a purse he made for *her* mom."

"Little did I know I was dealing with such lucky individuals today to know of the artist, Milton. He was a friend who respected ivory and whale teeth."

"He lived in the town where my grandma lives." Almost bursting with pride, Kathy felt very connected with this mouse.

"Ah, so your grandmother lives in Fairhaven, Massachusetts then?"

"Yup." Her enthusiasm was contagious. Her eyes were dancing with happiness.

"Milton used the original methods of very sharp, pointy tools to carve pictures into the teeth of whales. Mostly, he depicted old ships in full sail. These are known as *Tall Ships*. Often, he scratched his designs on slices of whale teeth so he could turn them into pins, pendants, or even decorate the lids of purses known as Nantucket Bags.

"He was even commissioned to create a piece of scrimshaw for President Kennedy. The artwork was a likeness of the president that Milton had designed. The president had a home on Cape Cod, and often flew in and out of the New Bedford airport. Driving from there to the Cape, he would pass through Fairhaven, and the town decided to give him a gift. Challenges came about in handing the scrimshaw over to the president due to security. Eventually Milton presented the tooth by going to the airport in person, and waiting patiently. The president had such a good time getting to know Milton, that he told his wife, Jackie, she should meet him, too.

"When they did meet, she secretly commissioned Milton to do a Presidential Seal on a tooth that she could give to her husband. Growing up on Cape Cod as the president did, he knew many ancient mariner stories about whale's teeth and scrimshaw. He kept the scrimshaw on his desk as a cherished memento. When he died, that tooth was even buried with him.

"Scrimshaw would be a lost art today if it wasn't for the

use of bones from other animals, like camels, and a man-made substance that looks like ivory.

"Ivory is a sign of strength in some cultures. If you were a hunter a long time ago, and killed an elephant or whale, you were viewed as being very strong. Today, thankfully, we look at these endangered creatures with admiration and compassion. It's important to respect all forms of life, even the lowly mouse!"

The mouse chuckled to himself. Then he looked at the children and was genuinely sad that his time with them was coming to an end.

"I hope I have given you much to think about later in life."

Everyone understood it was now time to head off into the tunnel.

"Will we meet again?" asked Kathy with a tear in her eye.

"That depends upon you entirely. I'm not sure if you will make it back to the caves again, but if you do, we will certainly meet."

The children headed towards the tunnel opening now with new knowledge and a piece of bone in their pouches.

Kathy stopped and asked the mouse a final question.

"Can you tell us about the bone you gave us before we leave?"

"It is from a camel who used to stop here on its way to

another land. Camels can go long distances without drinking water, because they store so much of it at a given time. This is important because they live in the desert where there is no water for miles and miles. Much the same as how a camel can store water, humans can store knowledge and emotions.

"When this camel was about to die, it came for one last visit and asked me to pass along its bones to special people, people I felt were deserving. Since you have all been thinking long and hard over your decision to move forward, you deserve to have a piece of that bone for when next you feel life is too difficult.

"When you return home, all the gifts you've received in the caves can become part of your daily routine. Maybe you'll meditate with a stone each day. Maybe you'll carry one piece in your pocket to touch when you feel stressed. Perhaps you'll simply display the items in a bookcase, or on a shelf. What you do with these gifts is up to you individually. Trust they are each given in a spirit of friendship."

The mouse had spoken about their return home.

Home!

Even if they didn't question him about that, they all felt the tunnel they were heading into next could be the last one before reaching their longed-for destination.

Yes, they had wanted an adventure. Well, Peter did at least. And they all went along with him.

But how much adventure do you need in day?
They were about to find out.

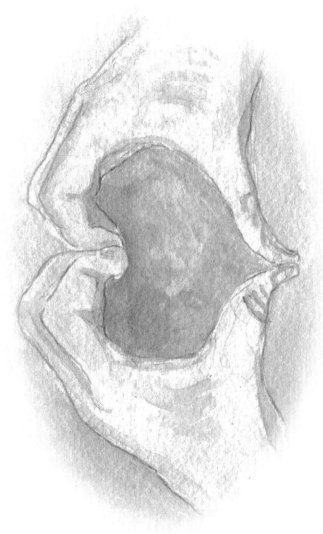

All the children now formed heart shapes with their hands.
They were happy and smiling.

Chapter Eight:
BIRTH

It wasn't the light in this tunnel but the music that caught their attention.

The music had started and stopped, stopped and started, throughout their journey. This time it continued playing as they walked deeper into the tunnel and now it was getting louder.

It created a rhythm the children soon found themselves walking in time to. When the music got a little faster, so did their pace. Justine even crawled and walked a little quicker.

Soon they were upon another cave opening.

Before entering, they stopped and listened.

"This is definitely where all the music has been coming from," said Peter.

"I like it," said Kathy as she bobbed in time. "Peter, do you like the music?"

"I know there's music, but without my hearing aids, I don't know if I can say if I wike it or not."

Kathy felt sad that Peter might not be able to enjoy music in the same way as everyone else.

Gwen said, "I like it. And I would like it even more if it got us home."

At that moment, Justine grabbed hold of Peter's pant leg and tugged. Peter sighed. He was tired and hungry, and could feel himself getting cranky.

"What, Justine?" Peter really didn't mean for it to come out sounding as though he was annoyed when actually, what he felt was despondency. "I'm sorry, Justine. I'm sorry to everyone. I just feel wike we won't ever get home again."

Gwen nodded in sympathy and said, "I think we are all getting tired, hungry, and cranky, but we have to go on, Peter. One of the things they have been telling us in the caves is that we must work together. That later we will remember what we have learned. If there's going to be a 'later' as they said, then that means we *will* get out. Maybe there's just this one more cave to go. Maybe the music is leading us note, by note, to the end of our journey."

Note by note. Step by step. This appealed to Peter and he smiled at them all. Well, it was a half-smile anyway.

Looking inside the cave, they saw a young lady, dressed in a long flowing gown, sitting at a harp. The blue-green color of the dress seemed to be glowing. Her harp was made of gold, and she was plucking at its golden strings. Her eyes were closed in deep concentration.

The children watched her hands move and glide over the strings, as she picked out a melody.

The music radiated through each child's soul.

Without opening her eyes, or interrupting her playing, she sensed the children had arrived. Her voice was as gentle as the music she was playing. "I am the siren song of turquoise."

"What's turkwoys?" Peter asked trying as hard as he could to pronounce it the way the lovely harpist had.

"Turquoise is the stone to use when you have had trials and tribulations while tackling problems," came the girl's soft melodic answer. "When no matter how many times you've tried to make a change, things don't work out as you hoped. Then, for no apparent reason, you try some new way, and suddenly, you feel different. That new response is a birth, or rebirth. You changed! Quite simply, it is a stone to use when you feel you are shifting from struggle, into a new place of clarity. It helps you get over that last hump and accept the shift in an easy, or graceful way."

Peter understood that. "You mean wike now, being in the cwystal caves, and not knowing the way back to our homes, and how we keep trying all the different tunnels to get us there?"

"Exactly. That's been part of your problem while here in the caves, finding a way out."

"Can't we simply ask you the way?" Gwen said hopefully, then realized there was more to ask. Her head was spinning. She couldn't even get out the second question just yet.

"I live here. There's no reason for me to leave. You see, I don't know the way out, nor do I want or need to go. For you, the problem is in your head, along with a possible answer to solve it."

The children spoke in unison. "In our heads? How can the way out be in our heads?"

"All problems begin in your mind first. You decide what to give energy to, and what to dismiss. When you make up your mind what is important to think about, and maybe even re-think about, you opt to make *that* the problem that needs a resolution. Often these problems become part of the heart muscle as well. This means you have given so much energy over to an issue, that you have become emotional about it. When you grow up, you'll meet people who do not make anything an issue in their lives. Those people seem to be golden. They trust that everything will work out, and usually it does. Those people can teach us all lessons. They make a decision, and if it doesn't work out, they trust that the next decision will be the right one."

Kathy had been so mesmerized by the harp playing she hadn't been following the conversation as closely as the others. She said, "I don't get it. What are you saying?"

That's when Gwen asked the second part of her question. "Wait, finding our way is *part* of our problem? What do you mean? What's the other part of our problem?"

Playing like she didn't have a care in the world, the harpist answered, "You each came into the cave of your own free will. It wasn't until the cave entrance closed behind you that you felt scared of not finding a way out. That was the beginning of how you started to pick on one another, and passed blame on whose fault it was.

"In some of the tunnels you met with opposition from one another, or other beings about getting out. You have been instructed to use your stones, pearls, and now bone, to help find peace, and perhaps a way out. Have any of you even got a stone out? Your pouches are laden down with new gifts that you have not begun to appreciate the way you should. Mother Nature has provided these stones, pearls, and bone to help people find a way through problematic times. You four are in one of those moments. Sit, find a stone, breathe deeply, and clear your minds. You haven't found your way out yet. With some healing power in your hands, trust that the next decision you make will be the right one."

Not arguing with the harpist, they found a place to sit, and followed her instructions.

Once a stone was chosen, they held it in their loosely clasped hands, and began to breathe deeply as they had been taught. Each child began to find a place inside that was peaceful. The beautiful harp music helped take them there.

Stress left them. Their breathing became deeper and more regular.

With eyes closed, they lost track of time, and didn't care. The only thing that was important right now was to find inner peace.

Peter was the first to open his eyes. Smiling at the harpist, he said, "Thank you."

Hearing his voice brought everyone else out of their meditative state. They opened their eyes and smiled. Peter was happy again.

Happy like he was on the slide in the pyramid.

Happy like when he joined in the singing.

Happy like he was when he played with the bubbles. And that made them all happy.

"What is it you are thanking me for, Peter?" asked the harpist, though she already knew the answer.

"Without much effort, you got us to sit and be calm. I feel as good as I do after a nap! You reminded us it's a good thing to use these stones, to hold and to think with."

The harpist stopped playing for the first time, opened her eyes, and studied her guests. "You each now have a piece of turquoise in your pouches."

Peering inside her pouch, Gwen said, "It looks like an egg. Not the right color, but egg shaped."

Giggling, Justine and Kathy were sitting with heads together looking at their new stones.

Peter held up a robin's egg blue piece of turquoise. It was also egg-shaped.

"Tell us again about turkwoys. About birth and rebirth."

"You have learned to communicate with Justine. That is a birth. You have learned how to talk to one another a bit better while being in here as well. That is a rebirth.

"Just before you came into my cave, you were tired, hungry, and even a bit cranky, yet no one lost their temper. You approached one another in a new way. That is the birth of a new understanding between you all. Everyone worked together to get inside this cave. All that shows a growth, and growth itself is birth. Emotional and mental birth has come to each one of you, and changed you in a good way. It's something that you will carry with you throughout your lives. Everyone in the cave is proud you have each gotten to this point. We have witnessed the birth of a new love between you, minds and hearts working together."

The children were calm and silent while pondering what they just heard. The harpist gently broke the silence.

"You have been thinking about the proper way out of the cave. Do you think you know the way out now?"

It took a good long minute or two before anyone responded. Casually, Peter glanced around this cave and was suddenly excited.

"I think I do."

Holding his hands up and placing fingers and thumbs together, he formed the shape of a heart. "Remember, this is the way we signed love to communicate with Justine."

He looked through the heart shape and his eyes came to rest on one particular tunnel. Excitedly, he pointed. The entrance to the tunnel was shaped like a heart. "It's got to be that way. Home is where the heart is. Where my parents love me and my sister."

All the children now formed heart shapes with their hands. They were happy and smiling. Justine giggled.

"You have thought over your problem of getting home, young man. When you felt inside that the answer was in front of you, you openly shared your excitement with your traveling companions. They shared in your glee. You just had a moment of birth. You passed it along to your friends, and that is an example of a ripple effect for good.

"With the turquoise in your hands, proceed with the joy of birth in your hearts, and remember, sharing knowledge for a common goal is always a good thing."

Glancing down into their hands once more, each child studied their piece of turquoise. It felt softer than some of the other stones they had been given. In a way, it felt a bit like the bone they all had. The color was very pleasant, too.

Looking up, they saw that the harpist, her golden harp, and her beautiful music had vanished like the last note of a song.

With each step by new step, they experienced the birth of a new confidence. They all walked towards the heart-shaped tunnel, each child holding on to their turquoise

knowing it would help them on the next leg of their journey—
one they hoped would lead them out of the cave.

Gwen began to sing. It was a popular tune from the radio
and it reminded them of home. Everyone joined in, even
Justine gurgled along. The words seemed so right.

"I have fun. We have fun. What happens when I am
young? I have fun! Now I am out. Who is there? We
are out. We are there..."

*Anxiety was again creeping over the children, when
a totem pole appeared in the center of the cave.*

Chapter Nine:
PARTNERSHIP

Singing carried them forward.

When one song ended, another took its place. They sang loudly, as if they no longer had a care in the world.

They put their turquoise back in their pouches and clapped along with the tunes they were singing.

Justine needed her hands to balance while she walked, so instead of clapping, she gurgled and cooed at the top of her voice.

They were happy.

Now they were no longer consumed by how short or long a tunnel was. When they finally saw a light ahead, they were convinced it was the exit to home.

But it wasn't.

It was just another cave. Another open space.

The singing stopped. The joy left them.

Even though disappointed, the turquoise they were carrying gave them *rebirth power.*

They would start their quest for home all over again in this new cave.

A pale blue glow let them see clearly around the perimeter.

There were no tunnel entrances to choose from. No exits to home.

Could this be a dead-end?

Anxiety was again creeping over the children when a totem pole appeared from nowhere.

Now, this was quite an accomplishment. The pole looked to be over fifty feet high.

It was black, white, red, blue, and natural colored wood. There were faces and bodies carved and painted all the way up.

At the very top was a bird-like face with a beak, and underneath that, wings that had a span of at least ten feet.

It looked fearsome. Totally fearsome.

Between this alarming structure before them now, and the thought they were trapped in a dead end, the children were understandably on edge.

"Knock-knock."

Whenever Kathy got nervous, she told knock-knock jokes. Usually they didn't make any sense. But they always relieved the tension.

"Who's there?" asked Peter and Gwen together.

"Crystals."

"Crystals who?"

"Crystals, aren't you glad I didn't say bananas?"

Kathy was bent over laughing. No one understood the joke, but her laughter was contagious, and soon everyone was laughing along with her. It didn't matter that it was nervous laughter.

"That was very enjoyable, Kathy," said a deep voice that echoed and vibrated around the cave.

The totem pole was talking to them. Of course it was! Everything else in these caves had a voice, so why not a totem pole?

His voice came from the bird head. The giant wings beat as the pole spoke. Needless to say they were nervous, but listened to what he had to say.

"I am a Tlingit Thunderbird totem pole. My tribes hail from the American Northwest and Canada. The Tlingit people still value their totem poles, and the Thunderbird, as a symbol. I represent strength and power, and I control the upper world. My carvings and paintings symbolize specific legends, beliefs, and notable events from Tlingit history."

For just a beat, a little chuckle crept into the totem pole's voice. "Generally, the Thunderbird is straight laced, so it was nice to experience such laughter just now."

Kathy approached it with wide eyes and an open heart. She held her hands up in the heart shape sign Peter used to symbolize love.

Even from where they were standing, and looking all the way up, they could see the totem pole had a tear in one eye. Kathy thought that was sweet.

"Where are we?" she asked kindly.

Gwen was already getting a neck cramp from looking up so high.

Justine simply lay down on the ground on her back, so she could get a good look at the totem.

"You are at the end of your journey, or the beginning, however you might like to look at it."

Thinking this was some sort of riddle, Kathy laughed again and said, "You're so funny!"

In a sing-song way she repeated his words. "You are at the end, that is the beginning. You are at the end, that is the beginning."

Peter and Gwen didn't laugh so much.

What was it? The end of the journey? Or the beginning? Surely the totem pole wasn't telling them they might have to start out all over again?

Peter and Gwen reached into their pouches for a stone. It didn't matter which stone. The only thing that mattered was having a stone in their hands to rub. They needed to feel the healing peace that a stone would surely bring to them.

Spinning around, Kathy kept up her singsong until she fell over. She lay on her back and looked up at the totem. Without taking a breath, she rattled off: "I like you. You are big, like some of the trees in my yard. I can't see all the way up to the top of your head, but I like your wings. We got a white feather thing in another cave today. It was from an Indian who had feathers all over his head. You don't have any feathers on your wings. How come?"

The totem pole waited a moment before answering, just in case Kathy was going to fire off any more questions. She remained silent, so he spoke.

"I do not have feathers because I am made of cedar wood, not unlike the trees in your yard. Someone carved me to portray the images you see before you today. My people use totem poles to symbolize many things. Some have carvings to represent the family history. In that case, you could call them *heraldic*, or family crest designs. Since we are tall totems, our most important stories or symbols are usually closest to the ground, where people can easily see them. In my situation, it's the top image of the raven that is most important. I am considered the most powerful spirit, able to swoop out of the sky, grab a giant whale from the oceans, and fly off into the mountains to eat my catch. That's a legend of course, but those kinds of legends are valued by my tribe because they always have a deeper meaning."

"We learned about whale's teeth in another cave!"

Like her close encounter with the mouse, Kathy spoke freely to the totem pole.

"Yes, I know, Kathy. Right now, I'd like to tell you more about my existence here. Some totems are constructed as welcome poles, especially to greet visitors. Others can be built to welcome someone into the afterlife, perhaps the same way you would use a headstone at a cemetery. The strongest form of totem is made to mark the family, and as I said, a story that goes along with their history. When totems are built out of cedar tree trunks, they last a very long time. They are naturally resistant to rot, and aren't normally affected by insects or the weather."

The totem pole paused before making his next important point. The children were about to learn another lesson.

"Long-lasting cedar is like your relationships. Surviving this day, in these caves and tunnels, with your friends, means that your friendships will most likely last a lifetime. Tlingit in my language means people...or people of the tides, since we usually live near water. Our tribe feels very strongly about the influence of family on our lives. Family can be people who are related to you by blood, or they can be people and animals that are very close to you throughout your lives. You will discover there are times when you and a very close friend might fall out of friendship. Maybe you have a disagreement. Maybe you simply get busy and forget to call or pay a visit. One week turns into a month, which then turns into a year. If you are as close as you thought, time apart won't matter."

Peter had the camel bone in hand. He was stressed and confused as what to do to keep his sister and Justine safe in the presence of this over-sized pole. It looked like it could topple at any minute. His hair was standing straight up on end. Hopeful the bone would bring forth calm, Peter rubbed, and rubbed. Soon, it worked. His hair even came down into some form of normal.

Gwen held the turquoise tightly in her hand giving birth to an understanding of what she was hearing from the totem pole.

Justine and Kathy were happy being on the floor of the cave staring up at the talking totem. Kathy and her silly knock-knock joke had touched the totem's heart. Assuming there was one inside that carved tree trunk.

"I *always* talk to my brother and my parents—*every single day!*" insisted Kathy.

"Yes, Kathy," said the totem pole to his favorite (although even totem poles are not supposed to have favorites). "That closeness is wonderful, but as you get older, you might perhaps forget to call, or get too busy to remain in touch with the friends you are traveling with here today. When you are true friends, it won't matter how much time passes. When you do get back in touch, it will seem as though you just spoke yesterday. Except you will find you have more to talk about now."

Pondering this conversation, Peter and Gwen were beginning to relax. The grips on their stones became a bit looser. Their breathing was even. Noticing this, the totem began to speak directly to them.

"I'm very pleased with you two today. You were both very nervous when you first saw me, and then acted like you didn't want to anger me. I know totem poles can sometimes look terrifying. Yet you have chosen *not* to distance yourself from me or your friends. Instead, you are using your stones to find your place of inner balance."

Peter thought he detected a warm smile in the totem pole's voice.

"Each one of you is special. Each one of you has a voice that is important for the group as well as for yourself alone. When you are able to freely communicate your own needs, or offer help to others in need, you will find true partnerships. Being a totem, I am a partnership of designs that my creator felt were important for himself, as well as his family.

"I wish for you to find partnerships in your continued lives once you leave the caves. Today I pass along the perfect partnership stone. It is called aquamarine. This wonderful stone is a member of the beryl family. There are many colors of beryl, and some have specific names like emerald, which everyone knows is green. Aquamarine on the other hand, can be the light blue color of a clear pool of water. It can be a blue with a *touch* of green to it. Whatever color aquamarine you might end up with is not as important as how it can assist you. Aquamarine can help you form a partnership within yourself, by connecting your heart with your mind. When you can expand that partnership outward to friends, family, and life mates, wow! Learn how to communicate what is in your heart with what is in your brain, you can then clearly convey those thoughts to others. Your thoughts will then be given without expectation, and that helps create true partnerships. Sometimes you need to compromise, but when you have open communication, that compromise can work for you *and* your friends and partners."

The stone that had unexpectedly appeared in their hands was tubular in shape. It had a quiet, inner glow that was lovely to all. Turning it around and around in their hands to see the light reflect off the stone, each child was mesmerized.

"You found your way to my cave through hardships and joy. Each segment of the journey has managed to bring you all closer together as friends. You have a better understanding of what makes each one of you nervous, scared, curious, and dare I say, happy. This means you already have a grasp of aquamarine and partnerships. Understand what a friend needs in difficult times, give them emotional support, and you are in a partnership. Partnership is not simply sharing space with someone else. It is also understanding another person in difficult moments. Give emotional support when it's called for, or a hand up when someone falls down.

"Sharing these cave experiences will be something you remember throughout your lives. Even if you drift away from one another, you will find each other again and again as the need arises. When you do, it will be comfortable, and welcoming. Like putting on a warm sweater when there is a chill in the air. That is partnership. Now, I know you have been nervous about not seeing any choices for leaving my cave."

Gwen and Peter caught one another's eye without turning their heads, and looked as though they had been caught cheating on an exam. Justine and Kathy were still in their places on the ground staring up at the totem.

"When you entered the caves and the opening closed, you were closed inside—literally closed inside the caves, and as you have discovered, sometimes closed within your hearts, minds, emotions and outlook. With the lessons learned from all those you met along the way, and the discovery of the healing power of the crystals, pearls, and bones you now have in your pouches, you have opened up. Opened up and learned how to become free. Deep within yourselves and each other. You have done well. And now it is time to be *literally* free. Because now is when you find your way out of the cave."

Jumping up from the cave floor, Kathy ran to Gwen and Peter. Grabbing Justine, all four children turned into a big pig pile on the floor, rolling around with excitement.

"Do you believe it, we're going home!"

"I'm so happy we will see Mom and Dad again." Justine gurgled.

"Yea for the totem pole!"

But the totem wasn't there to hear their cheers. Or perhaps it was, but had simply disappeared from view.

Then came a crackling sound. A snap. A pop. Like very loud versions of their favorite breakfast cereal.

Daylight flooded the cave.

Their eyes adjusted to the sunlight streaming in. They stood up slowly and watched in awe as light bounced off the crystals forming an opening.

The mouth of the cave.

The way out.

The way home.

The fresh air felt warm and spring-like, rather than the fall day chill when they entered the cave.

Tiny pink petals dropped from above like confetti welcoming heroes home.

Silhouetted against the bright outdoors were their parents with outstretched arms.

Breaking free from each other, they ran towards their parents and the hugs they knew they would be getting.

They didn't even bother to check the ground for snakes. (Having confronted a giant giraffe, a stomping horse, a talking pickle, and a fifty foot talking totem pole, imaginary snakes no longer seemed quite so fearsome!)

What was important now was being with those they loved.

Adults and children all spoke at once. Kisses, and then more kisses were exchanged. Gwen pulled back from her parents' grasp and asked: "Where are the police, or fire people, Mom?"

It was just what Peter was thinking as well. He said, "Yes, weren't you worried enough about us to call the powice?"

Gwen's mother began, "Darling, when we were children, *we* went into the crystal caves. When you all suddenly went missing, we knew where you were. We remembered where we came out all those years ago, so we have waited for you here."

Needless to say, this came as a bit of a surprise to the children. Their parents had never spoken of crystal caves to them.

Peter, without his usual indignant tone, said, "But we've been gone a wong time. Weren't you worried enough to call someone?"

"You know, you have only been gone for minutes, barely an hour. Not long enough to inform the authorities."

None of the children could wrap their brains around that. Something must be wrong. Maybe their parents were stuck in a time warp. Their adventure had been long and arduous. How could they have been gone for less than an hour. It was impossible!

"Time in the cave is relative, kids," said Justine's

mother. "We are sure it felt like a long time to you, but in reality, it was really no time at all."

Suddenly, understanding came to them as they held onto their pouches and merely thought about the stones inside. They looked into one another's eyes and smiled.

Of course.

The time in the cave was theirs and theirs alone. Out here in the real world, life operated differently.

Peter's mom placed his hearing aids in his ears, smoothed his unruly hair, and said to Kathy, "I see you left a sock and shoe behind in the cave, darling. I wonder if when you are twenty-one, you will still be going without shoes and socks!"

Their father spoke then.

"You see kids, this home has been in our family for generations. Family after family have lived here for longer than anyone can remember. It has been proven that whoever goes into the cave together, comes out as life-long friends. We keep the cave safe by not selling the property, or our home."

Motioning in a circle with his right hand, Peter's dad continued: "We have been friends since our adventure. We hope you all will be life-long friends now as well."

"The cave is magical," Justine's mom exclaimed. "But our parents never spoke about it, and felt uncomfortable when we did. Eventually, we gave up talking to them about our adventure, and kept the experience to ourselves. Maybe now though, we *can* talk about the cave and share our encounters."

"Yes, and share how the cave may have changed over the years, and then how the cave changed all our lives forever," said Gwen's father. "Maybe with the help of our turquoise stones, today will be the birth of a new understanding. A new way of sharing information. Maybe this is a time for growing together instead of the way our parents kept their experiences to themselves."

The adults gave out more hugs and kisses. Not only to their own children, but to each other's children.

Then the adults hugged one another. They were overjoyed to have their children back of course, but now there was the possibility they might learn things about the crystal caves their own parents never talked about.

Walking towards the house, that familiar harp music seemed to radiate through each child's soul again. They turned just in time to see the cave opening begin to close. They watched in stunned silence as the cave mouth curled up in the shape of a huge smile. The crystals that had been at the corners of the cave glinted in the sunlight adding a sparkle to the gigantic grin. The music faded into nothingness, and the cave finally sealed itself shut. All signs that it existed, gone.

Would it gone be forever?

They stared quietly at the spot where the cave opening had been. Then their own smiles and laughter returned.

Linking arms, they turned once again and continued to the house.

Feeling that invisible eyes were staring at them from behind, Peter pulled away and looked over his shoulder. His smile grew wider as he nodded his head, gave a thumbs-up sign to whoever, and whatever, was watching them unseen.

He then quickly ran after the others but not before kicking at the fallen leaves. There might not be any snakes but it gave him an idea.

When he caught up, he said to his sister, "Hey, Kathy, I've got a joke too…Knock, knock."

"Who's there?" she answered.

"Leaf."

"Leaf who?"

"Leaf with me now and we'll get hold of the zucchini bread before the others get back to the house."

Peter grabbed Kathy's hand and they ran off laughing. Everyone else laughed too and took off after them.

...it's never
The
End

...when you are willing to learn from stones, crystals, and organic materials like bone, shell, or pearls in life. There is always room for new understanding. So don't find an end, but rather a beginning. Enjoy your own self-discoveries, birth, as well as a partnership in new friends and concepts for life.

Some More Thoughts

Paying attention to my dreams is how I get through life. Hearing dream messages as they woke me numerous nights in a row, I was driven to write this book before I thought it ought to be done.

Making fine jewelry has been a passion that began as a child, and will carry me forward until death, I hope. Working with different karats and colors of gold with stones, crystals and pearls are some of what has brought me into the writing world.

I began with a book on my jewelry designs. It's called *Dreams Made of Stone*, and is about the healing properties of different stones, along with the symbolism of my designs.

I wrote a companion book with only healing properties I channeled, no photos. It's something you can leave in your car to discover why you were drawn to a certain stone you just saw somewhere. That book is called, *Stone Magic*.

From there I wrote a book that is loosely based on my travels in the world of fine art and craft shows. This novel is named, *Stepping Stones*, and is also about jewelry and stone properties.

Finding stones in the back yard as a child got me going on a collection that has brought me forward throughout life. If you only remember one thing from this page, please pay attention to the children in your world in their developing years...what they do, and where their interests lie, can tell you what direction they might go in life.

For me as a child, there were no women in the jewelry industry, so there was no way for my parents to see how to encourage me in that direction. Certainly, women were not in the field of cutting stones back then, either. Yet, through my interest in stones I have not only worked diligently on a career, but have also channeled stone healing properties, as well as written books about them. Along those same lines, I have watched the jewelry industry overflow with women throughout my career.

If anyone had paid close attention to my focus, they could have given me permission to follow my heart in this field of jewelry design. Passion is worth pursuit even if it doesn't seem possible to those around you. Imagine a world where all parents encourage their children to go after their dreams!

This book may give you the impetus to see what your child is paying attention to in their younger years!

Not that I want to sound preachy, I simply wish for all children to have open, creative minds, that carry them forward in life. If your dream doesn't bring in the financial gain you always hoped for, at least your heart will be happy!

Also, please find a stone to work with in both meditation, as well as a way to calm yourself in times of worry, or difficulty. Mother Nature has given us stones after all. The least we can do is make use of, and appreciate them!

Acknowledgements

Please know that this book has come into existence with the help and some insights of children who are living in my personal world.

I thank each and every one of them for their assistance in developing the characters I wrote about. Importantly, each character is not a carbon copy of these children. Through observation, as well as a few stories told by their parents, and grandparents, I have come to see each character develop in certain light.

Hopefully I have caught some of their fun and individual sides along the way. Perhaps, some of the not so nice manners we all communicate with one another can serve as gentle reminders that life is about learning through struggle.

Don't take everything written personally. The story is where the character development needed to go in order to make certain things happen.

Sam, Olivia, Parker, Adelaide, and Eliyanna have all contributed to this story. I thank you very much!

Lynn Hughes brought the visuals to life for the book. She is a talented artist who lives in Rhode Island. I have had the honor of selling her art through the gallery I owned in Newport. Getting to know her over time, I was very pleased she accepted the challenge of creating art for each chapter. Thank you.

Pam Potter has been my editor over four books and has a lot of experience in the world of metaphysics. Her insights have been of great value to me as I wrote and developed each book. Thank you.

William Armitage transformed my manuscript from a word document into what you see before you today. His additional edits and artistic magic designing the book cover, website, and *Crystal Caves* social media was a great gift. Thank you!

ABOUT THE AUTHOR

Candace L. Sherman is a stone whisperer who lives in Newport, RI. Her life-long passion for stones began in early childhood, as did her gift for making jewelry.

She opened a storefront in 1976 to sell her one-of-a-kind fine jewelry creations. Candace quickly became known for her ability to look at stones and know how they wanted to be mounted.

Through that store, her crystal shop, and her travels with fine art and craft shows, she taught others to work with stone healing energy and color vibrations.

Focusing on her ability to channel stone healing properties, she is now sharing her knowledge through books.

Made in the USA
Columbia, SC
26 May 2018